"*Revelation 911* arrives not a moment too soon, offering an anointed and theologically sound view of biblical prophecy within the modern world in which we live. This is possibly the most precisely timed book for a specific generation ever written. Birthed in a vision Paul Begley received from God, *Revelation 911* expounds on the book of Revelation in a relevant and thought-provoking manner. I really don't think there is an issue facing the church in our time that is not addressed. I have known Paul for years and I can hear his voice and his heart for the harvest in every word. For those who seek to understand Bible prophecy against the backdrop of today's global stage, *Revelation 911* is an essential read. Begley and Anderson guide you through a journey that is as enlightening and encouraging as it is urgent. God chose you and I to be alive in this moment. There is no plan B. It is us. We need to be prepared. We need to know what is coming. *Revelation 911* is your clarion call to open your eyes and let God show you what is really going on. I am truly honored to highly recommend *Revelation 911*. You will never be the same."

—**Larry Ragland,** pastor of Solid Rock Church in Birmingham, Alabama, host of *The Big Picture* TV show and online video series, and author of *I See Greatness in You*

"*Revelation 911* is a book every person looking for answers in Bible prophecy should have. I literally could not put it down! This is the definitive book on Bible prophecy you have been looking for."

—**Dr. Paul McGuire,** senior pastor of Paradise Mountain Church International and host of *The Paul McGuire Report*

"This compelling work offers a unique perspective on the profound subject of the end times, encompassing both biblical wisdom and contemporary insights. Pastor Paul Begley's deep understanding of Scripture shines through with his attention to detailed research and insightful analysis. With clarity and reverence, he guides readers through the intricate tapestry of end-time Bible passages. His ability to simplify complex concepts is truly remarkable, making this book a treasure for both seasoned believers and those new to the study of Bible prophecy. *Revelation 911* is a must-read for anyone seeking a better understanding of biblical prophecies and their relevance in today's world. Begley's acumen, combined with his compassionate approach, make this book an invaluable resource for those seeking truth, hope, and guidance in these tumultuous times. May this book help guide you on your own journey of faith as we draw closer to the coming of the Lord."

> —**Stevie Leydig,** pastor at the Tri-State Ministry Center in Hyndman, Pennsylvania

"Troy Anderson and Paul Begley knock it out of the park with *Revelation 911*. Regardless of one's eschatology or theological perspective, this must-read book offers profound and unique insights that bring Scripture and the headlines of the day into focus like never before. Don't miss this excellent book!"

> —**Alex Newman,** senior editor at *The New American*

"I am so glad that Paul and Troy have written this book. End-times events are happening all around us, and millions of people are looking for answers. This book addresses some of the hottest topics that people have questions about right now. I hope that as many people as possible will read it. We truly are living in the last days, and things are only going to get crazier from here. This book is explosive, and it will certainly get a lot of people talking. I appreciate Paul and Troy so much, and I think that you will really enjoy what they have to share."

> —**Michael Snyder,** founder of *The Economic Collapse* blog

Revelation 911

Revelation
911

How the Book of Revelation Intersects with Today's Headlines

Paul Begley
Troy Anderson

SALEM
BOOKS

an imprint of Regnery Publishing
Washington, D.C.

Scriptures marked ESV are taken from ESV ® Bible (The Holy Bible, English Standard Version®), copyright © 2001 by Crossway, a publishing ministry of Good News Publishers. Used by permission. All rights reserved. Scriptures marked KJV are taken from the King James Version, public domain.
Scripture quotations marked NIV are taken from the Holy Bible, New International Version®, NIV®. Copyright © 1973, 1978, 1984, 2011 by Biblica, Inc.® Used by permission of Zondervan. All rights reserved worldwide. www.zondervan.com. The "NIV" and "New International Version" are trademarks registered in the United States Patent and Trademark Office by Biblica, Inc.®
Scripture quotations marked NKJV are taken from the New King James Version®. Copyright © 1982 by Thomas Nelson. Used by permission. All rights reserved.
Scriptures marked NLT are taken from the Holy Bible, New Living Translation. Copyright © 1996, 2004, 2015 by Tyndale House Foundation. Used by permission of Tyndale House Ministries, Carol Stream, Illinois 60188. All rights reserved.
Scripture quotations marked NRSVA are taken from the New Revised Standard Version Bible: Anglicised Edition, copyright © 1989, 1995 the Division of Christian Education of the National Council of the Churches of Christ in the United States of America. Used by permission. All rights reserved.

Salem Books™ is a trademark of Salem Communications Holding Corporation.Regnery® and its colophon are registered trademarks of Salem Communications Holding Corporation.

ISBN: 978-1-68451-534-9
eISBN: 978-1-68451-579-0

Published in the United States by
Salem Books
An Imprint of Regnery Publishing
A Division of Salem Media Group
Washington, D.C.
www.SalemBooks.com

Manufactured in the United States of America

10 9 8 7 6 5 4 3 2 1

Books are available in quantity for promotional or premium use.
For information on discounts and terms, please visit our website:
www.SalemBooks.com

I (Paul) would like to dedicate this book to our millions of television and YouTube viewers over the years. Your faithfulness, prayers, and support have allowed us to continue the journey of bringing forth the end-time prophetic Word of God.

I would also like to dedicate this book to my wife, Heidi, who has stood beside me and encouraged me to keep pushing forward with the love we both have for the people of this world.

May this book change your life.

I (Troy) dedicate this book to my wife, Irene, who became seriously ill and was hospitalized for seventeen days as we were writing this book. The Begleys and their team prayed for Irene, along with our small group, Battle Ready Ministries, and our friends and family, and God saved her life.

I also dedicate this book to Jesus Christ, who gave Pastor Begley a vision regarding Revelation 9:11, urging him to alert the world that the events of the book of Revelation are "upon mankind."

CONTENTS

"The Hour Is Coming. It Is Upon Mankind."

They had as king over them the angel of the Abyss,
whose name in Hebrew is Abaddon and in Greek is
Apollyon (that is, Destroyer).

—Revelation 9:11 NIV

While praying and meditating on the book of Revelation in July 2021, I (Paul) was moved by the Holy Spirit into an open vision that revealed a series of mind-blowing apocalyptic events, unparalleled in human history, is approaching.

These events, foretold in the Bible, will so shake the world that the Apostle Luke foresaw people's hearts failing them for "fear and the expectation of those things which are coming on the earth" (Luke 21:26 NKJV).

In the vision, I saw a huge sign with red letters that said: "Revelation 9:11." Then the Lord said to me: "Revelation 9:11. It's about to happen. Warn the people."

I picked up my Bible and read Revelation 9. As I did, I realized that this often-overlooked chapter tells the story of a key being given to an angel who uses it to open the "Abyss"—a bottomless pit in which the worst of the beings cast out of Heaven alongside Lucifer have been kept chained.

The eleventh verse calls the king who comes out of this pit "Abaddon" or "Apollyon." In Greek, *Apollyon* means "Destroyer," and *Abaddon* describes a place of destruction.

When I read this, I thought, *Okay, this hasn't happened yet. I know Revelation tells us there are seven seals, seven trumpets, and seven vials of God's judgment poured upon the world, and I know the events in this book are not necessarily presented in chronological order. So where does this fit?*

The urgency of this message began to weigh heavily on me. I hadn't felt this kind of prophetic intensity in my spirit since the terrorist attacks on the World Trade Center and Pentagon that killed several thousand people on September 11, 2001. I felt compelled to warn the world of what the Lord had shown me.

Then the Lord said to me: "The hour is coming. The hour is coming. It is upon mankind."

The Coming Storm

Based on what God showed me, along with decades of research and investigation into the intersection of current events and biblical prophecies, we believe the world will soon experience a series of cataclysmic events, including those described in Revelation 9, that will pull back the veil between the heavenly and earthly realms, forever altering our understanding of the universe we live in.

Bible scholars have largely glossed over Revelation 9:11 for the last two thousand years, but this enigmatic biblical prophecy is one of approximately 2,500 contained in the Bible. Of those, about two thousand have already been fulfilled to the letter. The remaining five hundred pertain to current or future events.[1]

As the military-industrial complex is engaged in endless wars—Russia's invasion of Ukraine has renewed fears of global thermonuclear war, and geopolitical experts say China will likely attack Taiwan soon (potentially igniting World War Three)—we find ourselves in global peril.

War has marked most of human history, and now myriad weapons of mass destruction, including deadly biological ones, are in the hands of rogue states worldwide, increasing the chance they will be used with devastating results.

Scripture tells us that Satan—a master military tactician driven by unfathomable hatred of God—wants to destroy His creation with war, genocide, murder, greed, envy, and fear.

As Jesus Christ and His prophets foresaw, the demonic onslaught unleashed upon the planet in recent decades has set the stage for a global conflagration and catastrophic economic collapse, followed by the rise of the Antichrist and False Prophet who will preside over a world government, cashless society, and universal religion.

In this book, you'll discover not only the mind-bending ramifications of the ninth chapter of Revelation but gain a full understanding of the end times as described throughout Scripture.

Today, prophetic events are accelerating exponentially. Many people are concerned about the dramatic increase in extreme weather events and natural disasters that include mega-earthquakes, volcanic eruptions, tsunamis, record-setting heat, and floods. Meanwhile, we could soon be facing another devastating pandemic, are already battling the dangers of artificial intelligence, and are concerned that record levels of debt could trigger a global economic depression. People wonder whether the Great North American Eclipse forecast for April 8, 2024, could be one of the "signs in the sun, in the moon, and in the stars" (Luke 21:25 NKJV) that signals the beginning of a war, pestilence, natural disasters and other perils of the last days.

By the end of the seven-year Tribulation period, Revelation indicates most of humanity will have perished in a series of wars and calamities. What type of evil could cause this? Who is Apollyon (or Abaddon)? Where is the "Abyss" to which Revelation 9 refers?

What are the connections between transhumanism, artificial intelligence, the physics laboratory called CERN in Switzerland, secret societies, UFOs, extraterrestrials, the purported reverse-engineering of alien technologies, and biblical prophecies?

In the pages to follow, we'll explore what leads up to the opening of the Abyss, along with the end-times signs Christ told us to watch for in Matthew 24, Mark 13, Luke 21, and other parts of the Bible.

The "Great Reset" and "Agenda 2030"

This book will also prepare you and your family for the World Economic Forum's "Great Reset" plan and the United Nations' "Agenda 2030"—as well as the coming digital currency and "woke ESG corporatism" that is fundamentally upending not only the global economic structure, but human rights, personal freedoms, the ability to freely practice our faith in God, and even to pay our bills.[2]

We'll also share personal experiences that influenced both me and Troy—a Pulitzer Prize–nominated journalist who has spent a dozen years investigating whether we're on the cusp of many events prophesied in Revelation through hundreds of interviews with the world's foremost experts in geopolitics, intelligence, military affairs, economics, transhumanism, artificial intelligence, psychological warfare, and eschatology. He's also reviewed tens of thousands of pages' worth of governmental and academic documents and hundreds of books.

As we explore biblical prophecies and their link to world events, we will identify how global power is being consolidated, culminating in a one-world government controlled by the Antichrist and the False

Prophet. We will also discuss the Two Witnesses, follow the prophetic signs of the Four Horsemen of the Apocalypse, and delve into the Bible's greatest mind-twister: "Mystery, Babylon."

We will also learn about the "Great Harvest Revival" and how millions of people will come to salvation through the power of God before the end. This will bring about Christ's return to Earth, accompanied by the angelic armies of Heaven, to fight the final battle against the devil, the Antichrist, and False Prophet at Armageddon—defeating the powers of darkness and ushering Jesus's followers into an eternity of unimaginable wonders in the New Heaven, New Earth, and New Jerusalem.

"Under the Shadow of the Almighty"

Despite the grimness of the events foretold in Revelation 9:11, the rest of the Bible, including verses like Psalm 91:1, give us hope that God will bring us through whatever the future holds. This verse, known as "The Soldier's Prayer," says: "He who dwells in the secret place of the Most High shall abide under the shadow of the Almighty" (NKJV).

We wrote this book not only to alert people to what is coming, but to give you faith and confidence that God is in charge, and that drawing close to Him—as well as walking in the supernatural power, protection, and provision of the Holy Spirit—is the key to successfully navigating this tumultuous time in history.

If you don't already know Jesus, there is no time like the present to change that: Scripture clearly says that those who don't won't escape what Revelation says is coming. You certainly don't want to be like the people in Revelation 6:16–17 who say to the mountains and rocks, "Fall on us and hide us from the face of Him who sits on the throne and from the wrath of the Lamb! For the great day of His wrath has come, and who is able to stand?" (NKJV).

During the Tribulation, the elite will take shelter in underground bunkers to escape the chaos of what's happening above ground, but they won't be able to escape the wrath of God or the Great White Throne Judgment, when Christ decides the eternal destinies of unbelievers (Revelation 20:11–15).

If you haven't done so, now is the time to ask Jesus to forgive you of your sins and dedicate your life completely to Him, ensuring your eternal destiny is in Heaven. He created the universe and everything in it—and He loves you and has a plan for your life. God is very patient and "longsuffering toward us, not willing that any should perish but that all should come to repentance" (2 Peter 3:9 NKJV). Nonetheless, His prophetic timetable is unfolding, and will not be put off forever.

God's ultimate purpose in the Tribulation, as revealed in Scripture, is to deliver Christ's followers from a dying world full of sin, hate, murder, war, and catastrophic natural disasters while allowing a Christ-rejecting world to experience the suffering and sorrow created by the evil regime of Satan, the Antichrist and False Prophet; to bring millions of people to repentance; and to persuade millions of Jewish people—about a third of them, according to Zechariah 13:9—to put their faith in Jesus as their Messiah.[3]

In the vision he recorded in Revelation 7, the Apostle John describes seeing a "great multitude which no one could number" in Heaven after the Tribulation (v. 9 NKJV). He asked the angel who was revealing all these things to him about those "arrayed in white robes" (v. 9) and where they came from. One of the twenty-four elders stationed around the Throne of God told him: "These are the ones who come out of the great tribulation, and washed their robes and made them white in the blood of the Lamb" (v. 14).

Revival or Judgment?

Before and certainly during the Tribulation, hundreds of millions of people will realize that the Bible is the inerrant Word of God, that biblical prophecies are unfolding as predicted, and that God has indeed declared "the end from the beginning" (Isaiah 46:10 KJV). Many will decide to dedicate their lives to Christ. They will spread the Gospel and help fellow believers navigate the greatest persecution of Christians ever experienced on Earth.

This is the point at which we find ourselves today. On one hand, this is an exciting time to be a follower of Christ. God is calling us to join His army of warriors to help fulfill the Great Commission (Christ's instruction in Matthew 28:16–20 to take the Gospel to all the nations of the world) and the Great Commandment (His instruction in Matthew 22:36–40 to "love the Lord your God with all your heart and with all your soul and with all your mind" and to "love your neighbor as yourself").

The world is standing at the crossroads.

Now is the time to step forward in confident belief that "with God all things are possible" (Matthew 19:26 NIV) and fulfill the destiny God designed for us from the "foundation of the world" (Ephesians 1:3–14 NKJV).

As America has demonstrated many times, it's often in our darkest hours, while facing seemingly insurmountable odds—such as in the Revolutionary War, Civil War, and World War II—that courageous men and women rise to the occasion, and with God's help, push back the forces of darkness, achieving supernatural victory.

That time is here again. God has put the ball in our court. The destiny of America and the world is in our hands.

Part I

9/11

CHAPTER ONE

Ground Zero of the Apocalypse

Nine prophetic warning signs, and again, which I call
harbingers, appeared in the last days of ancient Israel
before its destruction that are now reappearing on America
soil—reappearing now as signs, as warnings, of a nation
heading away from God and heading to destruction.

—Jonathan Cahn, *The Harbinger*

In the year 2000, film producer James Fitzgerald received a pro-phetic warning from God about a "divine judgment" about to strike America. That summer, he rented the Madison Square Garden marquee to display that warning. The following year, terrorists hijacked planes and flew them into the World Trade Center.

Fitzgerald later wrote that the 9/11 attacks were

> God's instrument to begin the end-time events that lead to the second coming of the Lord. This audacious attack had set in motion two of the most critical end-time prophecies in the Bible: the beginning of sorrows and the judgments of the book of Revelation.[1]

The phrase, the "beginning of sorrows," comes from Matthew 24–25, known as the "Little Apocalypse" because of its parallels to the book of Revelation. In the passage, Christ's disciples ask Him about signs of the "end of the age."

> And Jesus answered and said to them: "Take heed that no one deceives you. For many will come in My name, saying, 'I am the Christ,' and will deceive many. And you will hear of wars and rumors of wars. See that you are not troubled; for all these things must come to pass, but the end is not yet. For nation will rise against nation, and kingdom against kingdom. And there will be famines, pestilences, and earthquakes in various places. All these are the beginning of sorrows.
>
> "Then they will deliver you up to tribulation and kill you, and you will be hated by all nations for My name's sake. And then many will be offended, will betray one another, and will hate one another. Then many false prophets will rise up and deceive many. And because lawlessness will abound, the love of many will grow cold. But he who endures to the end shall be saved. And this gospel of the kingdom will be preached in all the world as a witness to all the nations, and then the end will come." (Matthew 24:4–14 NKJV)

In late 2011, Fitzgerald encouraged me (Troy) to interview Rabbi Jonathan Cahn ahead of the release of his book *The Harbinger*. I did, and wrote several stories based on that interview for various media outlets.

I went on to interview Cahn on a regular basis over the following decade, believing the Lord had given him an important message for humanity.

The Harbinger details how the same nine signs of judgment that ancient Israel experienced before its destruction 2,600 years ago are reappearing in America today. Cahn told me,

The pattern of judgment is that . . . after calling and calling and calling on the nation turning away, He allows it to be shaken. He allows an enemy to make a strike on the land. That happened in ancient times [to Israel] and it happened in modern times with America. It happened with 9/11. God allowed that. That was a shaking.

The Lord gives the nation a window of time to come back to Him, to either repent or go toward revival, or to go away from God and head to judgment. We are now in a time where we have increasing signs that the window is coming to a close and if and we don't come back to God, we head to judgment, so this is crucial. America needs revival. It's not just a nice thing. It is the future of America. It's life and death.[2]

From 9/11 to Revelation 9:11

Like the surprise attack on Pearl Harbor on December 7, 1941, September 11, 2001, is a day that will "live in infamy."

Were you alive in 2001? Do you remember that day? Where were you when you found out what had happened? How did you feel when you saw the televised images of black smoke rising from the Twin Towers, people running for their lives and jumping from the upper floors of the skyscrapers to escape the infernos inside the buildings? Did you wonder about the people who were crushed when the towers fell, whose bodies were never found?

Do you recall the moment when you realized America was under attack? Do you recall the dread, the fear, the unknown? Was America going to be hit from every direction, in all its major cities? Was your heart beating out of your chest? Do you remember the shock and insecurity of it all, the unbelievable feeling that this couldn't possibly happen in America? Did it seem that something apocalyptic was happening?

The 9/11 attacks left an indelible mark on me (Paul) and the world, reshaping global politics, airplane travel, and international relations. The events of that day also were significant prophetically, setting the stage for the fulfillment of biblical prophecies, particularly those related to the destruction of "Babylon the Great" in the end times described in Revelation 18.

While there have been many interpretations of this passage, popular Bible commentator Henry H. Halley says it refers to the destruction of the "seat of Antichrist's political and economic power"—perhaps a "corrupt form of capitalism that eventually brings destruction to the world."[3] While some Bible scholars say "Babylon the Great" may refer to Europe, Rome, Mecca, or even ancient Babylon being first rebuilt and then destroyed in the end times, many point out its similarities to New York City (Wall Street, the global center of trade) and that America (the world's preeminent political and military power) could be destroyed in a single hour through a nuclear attack. In recent years, Russia, China, Iran, and North Korea have all suggested they have both the means and the ill will to attack the United States with nuclear weapons. After Russia invaded Ukraine in 2022, a poll conducted by the American Psychological Association revealed that nearly 70 percent of Americans are "worried that the invasion of Ukraine is going to lead to nuclear war, and . . . they fear that we are at the beginning stages of World War III."[4] Revelation 18:9–11 discusses this:

> "The kings of the earth who committed fornication and lived luxuriously with [Babylon the Great] will weep and lament for her, when they see the smoke of her burning, standing at a distance for fear of her torment, saying, 'Alas, alas, that great city Babylon, that mighty city! For in one hour your judgment has come.'

"And the merchants of the earth will weep and mourn over her, for no one buys their merchandise anymore." (NKJV)

Does this tell us that America will be destroyed at some point before or during the Tribulation? Will the "kings of the earth" remain "at a distance" because America is radioactive after being hit by nuclear missiles? That's a possibility many prophecy experts have raised in recent decades.

The 9/11 terrorist attacks led to several major geopolitical developments, including the proliferation of extremist ideologies, increased tensions in the Middle East, and the emergence of new power players on the global stage. The wars in Afghanistan and Iraq, the Arab Spring uprisings, and the war between Israel and Hamas, along with the aforementioned Russian invasion of Ukraine, are all potential precursors of the apocalyptic events described in Revelation.

Advanced technologies (the internet, electronic banking, microchip implants, etc.) all play a role in the evolving prophetic narrative. The rapid spread of information, the rise of artificial intelligence, and global surveillance capabilities cause us to consider the passages in Revelation referring to the "mark of the beast" and a global system of economic control.

Revelation 9:11 describes the moment when the Antichrist—a world leader who makes a peace treaty with Israel—steps onto the world stage. But instead of peace, he brings war, famine, plagues, and death upon the earth. In the wake of these calamities come natural and cosmic disorder, with a mega-earthquake, the sun turning black, the moon turning blood red, and asteroids and comets pummeling the planet.

For most of my life, when I (Paul) read Revelation 9, I'd just think, *Okay, wow, that's bad*, and keep reading. The eleventh verse had never before jumped off the page like it did when the Holy Spirit told me, *Hey, you'd better stop for a minute. Do you understand this event? It will change the whole world.* If you can picture a scene from J. R. R. Tolkien's *The Lord of the Rings,* when Sauron's orcs are rampaging through Middle Earth, you'll get a feeling for the sheer horror this event will engender.

Nine in Ten Pastors See Signs of the End Times

Today, polls show that about 80 percent of evangelical Christians, as well as scores of prominent ministers and biblical scholars, believe we're living in the end times. A recent Lifeway Research survey revealed that nearly nine of ten pastors see at least some current events matching those Jesus said would occur shortly before He returns to Earth:

Most agreed that Matthew 24–25, Mark 13, and Luke 21 refer to current events, including

- the rise of false prophets and false teachings (83 percent),
- the love of many believers growing cold (81 percent),
- traditional morals becoming less accepted (79 percent),
- wars and national conflicts (78 percent),
- earthquakes and other natural disasters increasing (76 percent),
- and people abandoning the faith (75 percent).[5]

Another poll, commissioned by bestselling author Joel C. Rosenberg, revealed that 40 percent of Americans (about 103 million total)—including 7 percent of atheists, 10 percent of agnostics, 19 percent of "secularists," 28 percent of Jews, 37 percent of Catholics, 54 percent of Protestants, and 70 percent of born-again evangelical Christians—agree that the Russian invasion of Ukraine is a sign of biblical prophecies coming to pass. It also showed that

- Forty percent of respondents believe the COVID-19 pandemic is a sign of biblical prophecies coming to pass.
- Forty-seven percent believe a new nuclear deal with Iran "will make the world more dangerous."
- Sixty-eight percent believe "the Iranian regime wants to use nuclear weapons to carry out their repeated threats to 'wipe Israel off the map' and bring about a Second Holocaust."[6]

Four Horsemen of the Apocalypse

The Four Horsemen of the Apocalypse—the white horse (the Antichrist, "Great Reset," globalism), red horse (war), black horse (famine and inflation), and pale horse (death, plagues, and disease)—are about to be released, leading to the War of Gog and Magog mentioned in Ezekiel 38–39 and the Sixth-Trumpet War detailed in Revelation 9.

We saw the devastation and fear the COVID-19 pandemic wrought in 2020, with more than 767 million people becoming ill and seven million dying.[7] We witnessed Russia's brutal attack on Ukraine in 2022.[8] Meanwhile, Xi Jinping, who oversees the world's third most powerful military and has ambitions to make China the world's leading superpower by 2030, is threatening to invade Taiwan, an act that could bring that nation into direct conflict with the United States.[9] At the same time, Iran is on the verge of obtaining nuclear weapons.[10] In North Korea, dictator Kim Jong-un is working on an "exponential increase" of nuclear weapons.[11]

With all these dictators (who view the Biden administration as weak and ill-prepared for war) vying for power, the world has become a powder keg. A multifront war could break out at any time.

Retired U.S. Army Lt. Gen. William G. "Jerry" Boykin, who served as the U.S. Deputy Undersecretary of Defense for Intelligence under President George W. Bush, says, "The situation is such that we could see world war very quickly. . . . one accident, one misstep, could bring us into a nuclear war."[12]

Noam Chomsky, a political theorist and a professor of linguistics emeritus at the Massachusetts Institute of Technology and perhaps the world's most cited living scholar, agrees. In late 2022, he said, "We are now facing the prospect of the destruction of organized human life on Earth."[13] Meanwhile, a group formed in 1947 to analyze the threat of nuclear war moved the Doomsday Clock to ninety seconds to midnight. "We are living in a time of unprecedented danger, and the Doomsday Clock time reflects that reality," said Bulletin of Atomic Scientists President Rachel Bronson. This "is the closest the clock has ever been set to midnight, and it's a decision our experts do not take lightly."[14]

Meanwhile, scientists at Rutgers University warn that even a limited nuclear conflict involving less than 3 percent of the planet's nuclear stockpiles could kill a third of humanity within two years, and a larger nuclear war between Russia and the United States could kill three-fourths of the world's population, or five billion people, in the same time frame—largely the result of global famine and starvation resulting from a tremendous disruption of the climate and food supplies.[15]

The end of days isn't five hundred years away. We're in the middle of it now.

This passage offers a glimpse of what the world will be like when the Four Horsemen of the Apocalypse ride:

I watched as the Lamb opened the first of the seven seals. Then I heard one of the four living creatures say in a voice like thunder, "Come!" I looked, and there before me was a white horse! Its rider held a bow, and he was given a crown, and he rode out as a conqueror bent on conquest.

When the Lamb opened the second seal, I heard the second living creature say, "Come!" Then another horse came out, a fiery red one. Its rider was given power to take peace from the earth and to make people kill each other. To him was given a large sword. When the Lamb opened the third seal, I heard the third living creature say, "Come!" I looked, and there before me was a black horse! Its rider was holding a pair of scales in his hand. Then I heard what sounded like a voice among the four living creatures, saying, "Two pounds of wheat for a day's wages, and six pounds of barley for a day's wages, and do not damage the oil and the wine!"

When the Lamb opened the fourth seal, I heard the voice of the fourth living creature say, "Come!" I looked, and there before me was a pale horse! Its rider was named Death, and Hades was following close behind him. They were given power over a fourth of the earth to kill by sword, famine and plague, and by the wild beasts of the earth. (Revelation 6:1–8 NKJV)

Think about the stunning things that have occurred since the beginning of the COVID-19 pandemic in early 2020—the lockdowns, church closures, a global campaign urging people to take vaccines, and even quarantine camps in some countries.[16] Given the fact that the pandemic struck right during the 2020 presidential campaign season and the controversy surrounding the results of that election, many people have asked whether the pandemic was planned—a test run to determine if people will comply with outrageous edicts from an authoritarian global state. It was incredible to see how quickly much of the world went along with much of what the authorities demanded, willingly handing over their freedom.

In 2020, environmental attorney Robert F. Kennedy Jr., who at press time was running for the 2024 Democratic presidential nomination, argued that the COVID vaccines could give globalists "complete authoritarian control" of the world, saying,

> We are in the last battle. This is the apocalypse. We are fighting for the salvation of humanity. We all knew this was coming at some point. I never believed it would come in my lifetime, but here it is.[17]

Is he right?

World Economic Forum and Deep State Consolidating Power

Today, globalists are gaining more control over our lives and consolidating power like never before.

Who do we mean by "globalists"? One player is the World Economic Forum, founded by Klaus Schwab. He gained a great deal of notoriety when he released his book *COVID-19: The Great Reset* in 2020, not long after the pandemic erupted. The World Economic Forum is an international organization that "engages the foremost political, business, cultural and other leaders of society to shape global, regional and industry agendas."[18] That may sound innocuous, but in our opinion—one which is shared by many—the WEF is a key player in the globalists' plan to create a one-world government. It will be like

Nazi Germany on steroids, a technocracy boosted by artificial intelligence and other advances.

Then there's the Deep State—the vast network of career bureaucrats in the government who are not held accountable to the citizenry through elections. This includes, but is not exclusive to, key figures in the intelligence community, defense industry, and financial services and technology sectors who influence and enact government policy without the transparency of a congressional vote. Meanwhile, globalists believe that economic and foreign policy should be planned internationally, rather than allowing each nation to determine what is best for its people.

The World Economic Forum, Deep State, and globalists have consolidated their power as global debt has hit a record $300 trillion. According to S&P Global,

> This translates to $37,500 of average debt for each person in the world versus GDP per capita of just $12,000. Government debt-to-GDP leverage grew aggressively, by 76%, to a total of 102%, from 2007 to 2022.[19]

What does this mean for you? To sum it up, "Your income demands are up by 20 percent, whereas your leftover cash is barely up at all. That's essentially a disaster for your standard of living," writes economist Jeffrey A. Tucker. "In short, you've been robbed."[20]

In a nutshell, a small group of excessively wealthy globalists, often using taxpayers' money, have succeeded in using politicians and organizations such as the World Economic Forum, United Nations, and many others to take control of much of the world's resources and wealth—even entire countries—at the expense of the average citizens.

This is all tied to Schwab's Great Reset plan for capitalism—which essentially means the end of capitalism as we know it. The reckless printing of worthless greenbacks not tied to the gold standard has not only transferred money from average citizens into the hands of those like Schwab but has raised fears of widespread bank collapses.[21]

One of the things driving inflation worldwide is the fact that Russia and Ukraine combined export nearly a third of the world's wheat and barley. Therefore, the war in the "breadbasket of the world" is making food more expensive across the globe, threatening to exacerbate both food shortages and political instability in developing countries. As a result, the United Nations Food and Agriculture Organization projects that up to 181 million people in forty-one countries could soon face a food crisis.[22]

Revelation 6:6 (NIV) predicts this, saying, "Two pounds of wheat [will go] for a day's wages, and six pounds of barley for a day's wages, and do not damage the oil and the wine!" This means food prices will be so high that it will take everything a person can earn in a day just to buy enough food to eat.

"The world will writhe in the clutches of stabbing hunger," writes Dallas Theological Seminary professor Mark Hitchcock. "The global economic collapse and food shortage will set the stage for the Antichrist to move into position to begin seizing control of the world economy as described in Revelation 13."[23]

Meanwhile, Microsoft founder Bill Gates warned that the world hasn't done much to get ready for the next pandemic[24]—which many accuse him of helping to plan, along with COVID-19. Of course, he isn't the only expert sounding this alarm. In May 2023, World Health Organization Director-General Dr. Tedros Adhanom Ghebreyesus warned the world must prepare for another pandemic that could be "even deadlier" than COVID-19. "The threat of another variant emerging that causes new surges of disease and death remains," he said. "And the threat of another pathogen emerging with even deadlier potential remains."[25]

Israel Prophecy Tour: "Now It Is Going to Begin"

In 2018, a woman named Rhonda Empson, whom I (Paul) had never met, had a prophetic dream in which God told her, "When Paul Begley goes to Israel, then it will begin." The beginning of what? She couldn't remember when she woke up, but she posted a video detailing her dream to YouTube.

Empson saw me walk into the room with a very serious expression on my face. "I knew something very important was at hand," she says in the video. "And he came in and tapped me on the shoulder and said very sternly: 'It's time to wake up.' So, I knew that something very important was about to come."[26]

I had no idea that had taken place when my wife and I led a tour of Israel in November 2019. Upon arriving home, I heard for the first time about the COVID virus that was beginning to sweep through China. At about that time, people began contacting me to say I had to watch Empson's YouTube video.

In February 2023, we again led a group on a tour of Israel. On our first day there, a magnitude 7.8 earthquake struck Turkey several hundred miles away, killing more than fifty thousand people in one of the deadliest natural disasters in modern history. There were more than forty aftershocks of 5.0 or greater.[27] Because a fault line runs from Turkey to Beirut to Tel Aviv, many in Israel were concerned about large aftershocks locally. Later, while we were at the Sea of Galilee, the moon turned blood red. That can often happen during a lunar eclipse—but that was just a normal night.

The next night, half the moon turned red. A woman in our group woke up at 2:30 a.m., looked out her window and saw it, and took a picture of it.

Okay, I thought, *we've got a blood moon that's not scheduled. I'm in Israel. What's going on here?*

When we got back to Jerusalem, Israeli forces were surrounding a home where members of a terror group were holed up. Officers fired missiles at the building to flush them out (a technique known as the "pressure cooker") and a firefight broke out, leaving eleven Palestinians dead and 102 injured.[28] Later that night, helicopters flew over our hotel as I was recording my show on the deck, and I realized that Israel had become the prophetic pressure cooker of our planet.

On the last day of our trip, Palestinians shot and killed two brothers waiting at a bus stop. Civilians hunted the gunmen down, and Israeli Defense Forces killed them. Meanwhile, enraged Israeli citizens torched thirty Palestinian homes and more than one hundred cars. It was odd, because Israelis usually don't get involved in these sorts of altercations; they typically let the IDF handle terrorism.[29]

Was this all just a series of coincidences, or was God saying, "Now it is going to begin"?

CHAPTER TWO

Understanding Future Events from Fulfilled Prophecies

And so it has been from the beginning of time. People have been obsessed with the desire to know what is going to happen in the future.

—Hal Lindsey, *The Late Great Planet Earth*

A s any good sleuth knows, fingerprints can be immensely powerful evidence. In the same way, the Old Testament contains hundreds of prophecies about the coming Messiah—and when biblical scholars piece together these ancient predictions, they create a fingerprint. The Bible says whoever fits this fingerprint is the Messiah.

"Of all the human beings who have ever lived on this planet, only Jesus Christ has been able to fit this prophetic fingerprint," says former atheist and *New York Times* bestselling author Lee Strobel.[1]

The Old Testament prophecies of the Messiah foretold that He would be:

- a descendant of Abraham (Genesis 12:3, Acts 3:25–26, Matthew 1:1)
- of the tribe of Judah and the house of David (Genesis 49:10, Luke 3:23)

- born in Bethlehem (Micah 5:2, Matthew 2:4–6)
- heralded by a messenger of the Lord, who turned out to be John the Baptist (Malachi 4:5–6, Matthew 11:10–15, Isaiah 40:3–4, John 1:23)
- cleanse the Jewish Temple (Isaiah 56:7, Jeremiah 7:11, Mark 11:15–19, Matthew 21:12–17, Luke 19:45–48, John 2:13–16)
- killed at a specific time in history (Exodus 12:21–27, 1 Corinthians 5:7)
- rejected by the Jews (Isaiah 6:9–10, Matthew 13:13–15)
- pierced in His hands and feet (Psalm 22:16, John 19:36–37)

All this was predicted hundreds of years before crucifixion was even invented.

The Old Testament also predicted that He would rise from the dead (Psalm 16:9–11, Acts 2:31, Luke 24:5–7) and afterward sit down at the right hand of God (Psalm 110:1, Hebrews 1:3, Hebrews 12:2, 1 Peter 3:22, Acts 7:55–56). Isaiah 53 is a particularly pivotal passage: Written seven hundred years before Jesus was born in Bethlehem, it contains a dozen details about His suffering, death, and resurrection, and all of them were fulfilled.

Can the fulfillment of these prophecies be explained in any way other than God's foreknowledge?

Decades ago, as he was investigating the evidence in an effort to debunk the Christian faith, Strobel read *Science Speaks: Scientific Proof of the Accuracy of Prophecy and the Bible* by Dr. Peter W. Stoner, a professor of mathematics and astronomy at Pasadena City College. Stoner wrote the book when he realized that biblical prophecies could be quantified. In other words, if the Bible predicted the Messiah would be born in Bethlehem, he wanted to quantify how many people in history have been born in Bethlehem so he could determine the odds that any human being born in Bethlehem could fulfill other prophecies about the Messiah.

So, Stoner and about six hundred of his students made conservative calculations of the odds that any human in history could have fulfilled just eight of the more than three hundred prophecies about Jesus in the Old Testament, and determined it was one in a trillion to the twelfth power.[2]

"That's a big number!" Strobel said. "How can we understand that number? That would be like taking one atom . . . spray-painting it red, and then putting that atom somewhere in a space equal to a trillion, trillion, trillion, trillion, billion universes the size of our universe, and then blindfolding someone, putting him in a spaceship, and saying, 'You can fly among these trillion, trillion, trillion, trillion, billion universes, but you can only stop your spaceship one time and you can open up your little porthole just once, and you can stick out your little tweezers just one time, and pull in one atom.' What are the odds it would be the atom that had been spray-painted red? The same odds that any human being in history could fulfill eight of these ancient prophecies and I can tell you what—Jesus did it."[3]

The Unique, Predictive Power of the Bible

Unlike the world's other sacred texts, the Bible predicts future events with verifiable accuracy. The *Bhagavad Gita*, the *Koran*, the Hindu Vedas, the *Ramayana*, and the sayings of Buddha and Confucius contain relatively few predictions of the future, and those have dubious accuracy. On the other hand, the Bible's unblemished record of thousands of fulfilled prophecies authenticates it as the inerrant Word of God.[4] As author and Bible prophecy expert Dave Hunt points out:

No prophecies foretold the coming of Buddha, Muhammad, Zoroaster, Confucius, Joseph Smith, Mary Baker Eddy, the currently popular Hindu gurus who have invaded the West, or any other religious leader, all of whom lack the credentials which distinguish Jesus Christ. Yet there are more than 300 Old Testament prophecies which identify Israel's Messiah. . . . The fulfillment of these prophecies in minute detail in the life, death, and resurrection of Jesus of Nazareth demonstrates indisputably that He is the promised One, the true and only Savior.[5]

This fact led Hugh Ross, founder of Reasons to Believe—an organization that researches how discoveries about nature harmonize with the Bible—to faith in Christ as a young man.

"I was not raised in a Christian home, but as I was comparing the world's different religions and the holy books that undergird them, I noticed that they all made attempts to predict future scientific discoveries, but the Bible did this hundreds of times as opposed to a handful of times," says Ross, a prolific author with a doctorate in astrophysics. "Moreover, what you see in the Bible in terms of what it predicts about future scientific discoveries and future historical events is correct."[6]

Jesus's Testimony Is the Spirit of Prophecy

The Bible is overflowing with prophecies about both the first and second comings of Christ. Revelation 19:10 says, "For the testimony of Jesus is the spirit of prophecy" (NKJV). The New Living Translation puts it this way: "For the essence of prophecy is to give a clear witness for Jesus."

Here are some surprising statistics about Bible prophecy:

- Of 333 prophecies regarding Jesus, only 109 were fulfilled with His first coming, leaving 224 to be fulfilled by His Second Coming.

- The New Testament refers to Christ's return more than three hundred times, or one out of every thirty verses.
- Of the New Testament's twenty-seven books, twenty-three mention Christ's return at least once.
- Jesus Himself spoke of His Second Coming twenty-one times.
- For every mention of Christ's first coming, the Second Coming is mentioned eight times.
- People are told more than fifty times to be ready for Christ's return.[7]

"Jesus basically endorsed Bible prophecies as a way of establishing truth," Ross says. "One of the things I see in the book of Daniel, for example, is that when humanity comes into the time of the end, knowledge will vastly increase (Daniel 12:4). I think there's plenty of evidence we're living in those days. In my own discipline of astronomy and physics, the knowledge base doubles about every six years. Many [other] scientific disciplines [also] are seeing that exponential explosion of increasing knowledge."[8]

In addition, the Old Testament prophets Isaiah, Jeremiah, Daniel, and Ezekiel correctly predicted that God would judge the Jewish people for their sins, scatter them throughout the world, and bring them back together as a nation in the end times. This happened during the Babylonian Exile—when Jews were taken as captives to Babylon and held there for several decades in the sixth century BC—and later when Roman Emperor Titus destroyed Jerusalem in AD 70, selling many Jews as slaves.[9] Over the next two thousand years, large populations of Jewish people moved to Spain, France, Germany, Poland, Russia, and eventually the United States. After that lengthy diaspora, Israel was reborn as a nation on May 14, 1948.

Unbeknownst to much of the world, the Bible has correctly predicted thousands of "future historical events," Ross says. While he was still an atheist, he systematically went through the Bible, filling a ledger with notes of all the future events and scientific discoveries it accurately and specifically predicted.

He found that the odds of those things happening without divine intervention to be "less than one in ten to the three hundredth power."[10]

Reasons to Study Bible Prophecy

Beyond the fact that the Holy Spirit will transform your life and mind, helping you fulfill God's destiny for your life, there are many reasons to study Bible prophecy.

First, it provides concrete proof of the divine inspiration of the Word of God. As we've illustrated, it's a reliable source of advice for all aspects of life—and based on its perfect track record so far, we can be sure that its prophecies of the future will come to pass too. Tragically, many ministers today know little about Bible prophecy because it isn't taught at most seminaries. As a result, many don't teach prophecy from the pulpit, leaving many believers ignorant of God's exciting plans for their future. Saint Augustine once opined that the Bible's prophetic passages should not be taken literally—and as a result, many mainline and evangelical denominations today do not do so.

Secondly, Revelation gives us confidence that Jesus will return to Earth—our "blessed hope" (Titus 2:13)—bringing an end to evil and injustice. It is filled with inspirational details about Christ's thousand-year reign on Earth following the Tribulation, as well as the New Heaven, New Earth, and New Jerusalem (Revelation 21:1–2). It is the grand finale of the magnificent biblical narrative, foretelling Christ's ultimate triumph over the powers of darkness. This is important because as the world gets darker, our need to remain hopeful will intensify.

"Human beings can absorb many pressures in life, but a lack of hope is not one of them," Tim LaHaye and Thomas Ice write in *Charting the End Times.*

> The world in which we live has no hope. . . . The whole world yearns for peace, but knows no peace. Mankind's problems continually worsen, leaving many people without hope. Prophecy students, however, not only know what our loving God has planned for the future of this planet and the billions who live on it, but they also have a firm confidence toward the future and are not afraid. . . . This confidence or hope is not automatic; it comes in response to the study of the Word of God in general as well as those passages that pertain to prophecy. . . . Those who are familiar with Bible prophecy are the only ones who can face what seems to be an uncertain future with peaceful confidence.[11]

Thirdly, not knowing about God's prophetic plan leaves us vulnerable to the false teachings and deceptive ideologies that are so widespread today. When Jesus's disciples asked Him about signs of the end of the age, the first thing He said was, "Watch out that no one deceives you" (Matthew 24:4 NIV). He said many false prophets would arise in the last days who would deceive many, which will include those who are unfamiliar with the Bible and its prophecies (Matthew 24:4, 24).

The fourth reason to study prophecy is that it often lights an evangelistic passion in the hearts of many believers, as well as inspiring unbelievers to put their faith in Christ. The last Great Awakening in the United States—the Jesus Movement in the late 1960s and early 1970s—was significantly inspired by the end times, drawing momentum from Hal Lindsey's *The Late Great Planet Earth.* The movement, which largely began in Southern California, spread throughout the

United States and the world, helping bring millions of new believers into the body of Christ.[12]

Today, many people are frustrated by the wickedness in the world, especially hypocrisy within the Church. Yet, one tool God uses to inspire believers to live holy lives is the study of prophecy, especially passages regarding Christ's return. Consider what the Apostle John wrote: "And everyone who has this hope in Him purifies himself, just as He is pure" (1 John 3:3 NKJV).

Documentable Future Events

The Earth

Knowing these things, let's turn our attention to the future. Two thousand years ago, Christ predicted a series of natural disasters in the last days: "And there will be great earthquakes in various places, and famines and pestilences; and there will be fearful sights and great signs from heaven" (Luke 21:11 NKJV). The Apostle John tells us the greatest earthquake in human history will strike before the Battle of Armageddon:

> The seventh angel poured out his bowl into the air, and out of the temple came a loud voice from the throne, saying, "It is done!" Then there came flashes of lightning, rumblings, peals of thunder and a severe earthquake. No earthquake like it has ever occurred since mankind has been on earth, so tremendous was the quake. The great city split into three parts, and the cities of the nations collapsed. God remembered Babylon the Great and gave her the cup filled with the wine of the fury of his wrath. Every island fled away and the mountains could not be found. (Revelation 16:17–20 NIV)

Today, there are about 1,350 potentially active volcanoes on the earth's crust, and many more on the ocean floors. About five hundred of them already have erupted at some point, and many are located along the Pacific Rim's "Ring of Fire."[13] One of these is Hunga Tonga-Hunga Ha'apai, a submarine volcano in the South Pacific. Its August 2023 eruption was one of the most powerful blasts in decades, sending its ash into outer space.[14] Earlier that year, scientists discovered more than nineteen thousand undersea volcanoes, some of which can cause tsunamis if they erupt.[15]

Fifty miles off the coast of Oregon, scientists have discovered a giant hole—dubbed the "Crack of Doom"—spewing hot liquid into the Pacific Ocean that they warn could trigger a 9.0 earthquake with the potential to devastate the West Coast. The chasm is located along a six-hundred-mile fault line that stretches from California to Canada, known as the Cascadia Subduction Zone. One day, experts say, this fault will slide, bringing destruction even greater than the long-anticipated "Big One" along California's storied San Andreas Fault.[16]

After tracking the number of earthquakes worldwide for two decades, author Jeff Van Hatten has found that they've been increasing on an annual basis since 2012—and getting stronger. In 2021, the total number of earthquakes worldwide (159,633) was 11.25 times the average of 14,194 that took place between 1900 and the year 2000. Interestingly, that uptick began after the rebirth of Israel, in 1949.[17]

The Heavens

The Bible is full of references to asteroids and comets pummeling the planet, especially during the Tribulation. For instance,

> The second angel blew his trumpet, and something like a great mountain, burning with fire, was thrown into the

sea, and a third of the sea became blood. A third of the
living creatures in the sea died, and a third of the ships were
destroyed. (Revelation 8:8–9 ESV)

According to *The Prophecy Knowledge Handbook*, this verse may
refer to a "large object falling from heaven."

It was indicated earlier in the sixth seal that stars fell to
earth, and, apparently, it is not an impossibility, especially in
a supernatural situation like this, for a large material object
to fall into the sea. Such, of course, would be devastating as
it would cause mountainous tidal waves.[18]

Meanwhile, the sun has been exploding with massive solar flares
and coronal mass ejections that can affect the power and communications infrastructure here on Earth. According to a January 2023
Space.com article,

Since December 2019, solar activity, including the number of
sunspots and solar flares, has increased. The sun is heading
to the next solar maximum, in 2024, when the star's polarity
will reverse and many more active regions will appear.[19]

Experts say that increased volatility could explain the increase in
earthquakes and volcanic explosions we're seeing.[20]

Scientists also have discovered more than thirty thousand asteroids in our solar system are following a path that brings them close
to Earth.[21] Dr. Ed Lu, executive director of the B612 Foundation's
Asteroid Institute and a former astronaut, said these space rocks "are
thousands of times more numerous" than previously believed, and
scientists have only found a "small percentage" of them.[22] One is a

potential "extinction-level asteroid that could someday hit Earth," dubbed 2022 AP7, near Venus (an area that is difficult to see because of the sun's glare).[23]

Luke 21:25–26 says:

> "And there will be signs in the sun, in the moon, and in the stars; and on the earth distress of nations, with perplexity, the sea and the waves roaring; men's hearts failing them from fear and the expectation of those things which are coming on the earth, for the powers of the heavens will be shaken." (NKJV)

God is sending the world a 911 emergency call, saying, in effect, "Wake up!" When we witness these signs accelerating and converging, Jesus tells us what to expect:

> "Then they will see the Son of Man coming in a cloud with power and great glory. Now when these things begin to happen, look up and lift up your heads, because your redemption draws near." (Luke 21:27–28 NKJV)

CHAPTER THREE

Vortex of Evil

*Some of the biggest men in the United States, in the field
of commerce and manufacture, are afraid of somebody,
are afraid of something. They know there is a power
somewhere so organized, so subtle, so watchful, so
interlocked, so complete, so pervasive, that they had
better not speak above their breath when they speak in
condemnation of it.*

—*President Woodrow Wilson*

In 1784, a messenger from the Illuminati—a secret society founded
in 1776 by Adam Weishaupt, a law professor at Germany's
University of Ingolstadt—was struck by lightning while on his way
to Paris.[1] On the dead man's body, authorities discovered a docu-
ment written by Weishaupt titled, "The Original Shift in Days of
Illumination." It described the Illuminati's goal for a "New World
Order through Revolution" and mentioned details about the French
Revolution—which didn't start until 1787.[2]

Bavarian authorities later discovered more documents in Weishaupt's
home that discussed taking control of Freemasonry—and by extension, all the governmental groups Freemasons control—overthrowing
European monarchies and eliminating the Catholic Church. Weishaupt
wrote that he wanted to "raise liberty from its ashes—to restore man his

original rights . . . to obtain an eternal victory over oppressors—and to work the redemption of mankind, in secret schools of wisdom."[3] Some of his words could be mistaken for those of his contemporary, Founding Father Thomas Jefferson.

> Until Weishaupt's screed reaches a tipping point, calling for a secret society of initiates to lead the rebellion against authority, as opposed to the American leader's view of a broadly based public movement for freedom.[4]

Bavarian authorities rightly interpreted that as a threat, and began hunting Freemasons and members of the Illuminati. Weishaupt managed to escape, settling in Gotha—a city in a separate German state— with his family until his death in 1830.[5]

At the time, the Illuminati consisted of about two thousand young men of "wealth, rank, and social importance" as well as intellectuals who wanted to free themselves from "age-old chains of church and state." One of the most famous members was "literary giant" Johann Wolfgang von Goethe, who wrote *Faust*—a play inspired by the story of a German necromancer and astrologer who sold his soul to the devil in exchange for knowledge and power.[6]

Neither Weishaupt's thoughts nor his compatriots were confined to the European continent, however: Founding Father Thomas Jefferson not only

> defended Weishaupt's scheme for his fellow radicals to infil- trate Masonic lodges, whose secrecy would protect them, [but wrote] a letter to the president of The College of William and Mary, [that since] "Weishaupt lived under the tyranny of a despot & priests, he knew that caution was necessary even in spreading information, & [on] the principles of pure

morality. He proposed therefore to lead the Freemasons to adopt this object & to make the objects of their institution the diffusion of science & virtue."[7]

Though the Bavarian government banned the Illuminati in 1785, historical records contain no evidence that it actually disbanded. As·a result, this mysterious group has figured prominently in conspiracy theories for centuries, with many believing its members came to include the world's most powerful banking families, European royalty, American politicians, and other sectors of society worldwide, becoming exponentially more powerful and wealthy over the years.

No one can prove or disprove these theories—but at the very least, the ideas of the Illuminati have inspired the concerted campaign for a "new world order" we see coming from globalists today.

Illuminati and Freemasonry

In his book *The Illuminati: The Secret Society that Hijacked the World*, the late Jim Marrs, an investigative journalist and *New York Times* bestselling author, wrote that in the late 1700s and early 1800s, the Illuminati merged with Freemasonry. That made them verifiably the world's largest secret society, with an estimated two to six million members.[8]

In fact, it's so secretive that even a lot of Freemasons are still in the dark about what takes place in its upper echelons. The vast majority of American Freemasons look upon their brotherhood as little different than that of the Lion's Club, the Optimists, or the Chamber of Commerce. And from their standpoint, this is true. Masonic literature makes clear that only those initiates who progress beyond thirty-three-degree status are educated in the group's true goals and secrets. . . .

To deny any relationship between Freemasonry and world events, one almost must ignore the infusion of Illuminati doctrine into Freemasonry in the late 1700s. Such infusion included the philosophies of Georg Wilhelm Friedrich Hegel and Weishaupt, which included "the end justifies the means" and "to achieve synthesis requires two opposing forces." It is clear that Illuminized Freemasons have used any and every opportunity to advance their cause regardless of which side they may support at the moment. The famous Masonic slogan *Ordo ab Chao* (Order out of Chaos) is generally regarded as referring to the Order's attempt to bring an order of knowledge to the chaos of the various human beliefs and philosophies in the world—a new world order.[9]

Yet Freemasonry is just one secret society in a network of organizations that have quietly gained tremendous influence at the highest levels of government, media, business, religion, and academia over the centuries. To name just a few, this broader network includes:

- Yale University's Skull and Bones fraternity;
- the Bohemian Grove—a private club in San Francisco and Sonoma County;
- the Bilderberg Group—a collection of powerful European and American policymakers and other elites who began meeting annually in 1954 on the premise of devising ways to prevent a third world war;
- the Royal Institute of International Affairs—a British think tank founded in 1920;
- the Council on Foreign Relations (CFR)—the American counterpart to the Royal Institute of International Affairs, founded in 1921;

- the Trilateral Commission—a nongovernmental organization founded in 1973 by American philanthropist David Rockefeller, former President Jimmy Carter, and former U.S. National Security Advisor Zbigniew Brzezinski to bring Japan into the relationship between Europe and North America;
- the Club of Rome—an informal group of intellectual and business elites founded in 1968 who meet to discuss global issues;
- the United Nations—the intergovernmental organization founded in 1945;
- the World Economic Forum, which we've already discussed;
- and many other organizations and foundations.[10]

Collectively, this is the modern iteration of groups like the Bavarian Illuminati, Rosicrucians, Knights Templar, Assassins, Druids, Pythagorean Brotherhood, and others dating back thousands of years to the "mystery religions" of ancient Rome, Greece, Egypt, and Babylon.[11] As Jean-Pierre Isbouts wrote in a special edition of *National Geographic* devoted to the topic,

> Secret societies have been an integral part of human civilization from the dawn of time to the present day. They have toppled rulers and reshaped nations; influenced writers and artists; and changed the way we think about God.[12]

"New World Order" Rising

Today, the world is caught in a vacuum of evil, ushering humanity into the "new world order"—a global government with one economy and a single religious system that the Bible says will be ruled by the Antichrist and False Prophet (Revelation 13).

World leaders, including Nazi dictator Adolf Hitler, British prime minister Winston Churchill, and American presidents Woodrow Wilson, George H. W. Bush, and Joe Biden, have often called for a "new world order."

"Now is a time when things are shifting," Biden told a group of CEOs from General Motors, Apple, and Amazon in 2022. "There's going to be a new world order out there, and we've got to lead it. And we've got to unite the rest of the free world in doing it."[13]

At the secretive Trilateral Commission's first global plenary meeting in India in March 2023, a speaker (who cannot be identified according to commission rules) said, "This year, 2023, is Year One of this new global order."[14]

Meanwhile, the CFR recently asked foreign policy experts to rank the top global threats, including the danger of nuclear war. The CFR is an elite private club that "functions as the brain trust, command center, and public face of the Deep State" whose globalist members fill top posts in Big Government, Big Business, Big Media, Big Tech, Big Labor, and Big Pharma.[15] Its report, which highlighted China, Russia, North Korea, and Iran as the biggest threats to America, Israel, and other Western nations,[16] came as Russian President Vladimir Putin and Chinese President Xi Jinping held a two-day meeting last spring during which Xi "made a strong show of solidarity" with Putin.

"Now there are changes that haven't happened in (one hundred) years," he told Putin. "When we are together, we drive these changes."

"I agree," Putin said, to which Xi responded: "Take care of yourself dear friend, please."[17]

Given that Xi and Putin control the world's second and third most powerful militaries after the United States, Earth is becoming an increasingly dangerous place. Xi recently brokered an historic peace accord between Saudi Arabia and Iran, reestablishing diplomatic relations between Tehran and Riyadh after seven years of rancor—catapulting China into the role of a "global truce broker."[18] This left Israel, which was attempting to broker its own deal with Saudi Arabia while it teeters on the verge of war with Iran, as the odd man out.

These stunning developments have strengthened ties between nations the Bible indicates will form an alliance to attack Israel during the last days (Ezekiel 38:8). Ezekiel 38:1–6 lists the countries that will invade Israel, identifying them by the ancient names still in use when the book was written. Bible scholars identify them as modern-day Russia, Iran, Turkey, and other countries in the Middle East, and conclude that the invasion will likely occur just before or within the first half of the Tribulation, while Israel is protected by a peace accord struck with the Antichrist.

Then, just when it seems Israel will be destroyed, Ezekiel 38:18 says God's "hot anger will be aroused," and He will rescue His people by causing a great earthquake (vv. 19–20). There will also be infighting among the Russian-led coalition (v. 21), disease outbreaks (v. 22), and torrential rain, hailstones, and burning sulfur (v. 22) that will super-naturally destroy the Russian-Islamic coalition.[19]

While China isn't specifically listed in this passage, Revelation often speaks of the "dragon"—which figures prominently in Chinese symbolism—as well as the role "kings from the east" will play in Latter Days events (Revelation 16:12).

While some prophecy experts say the Abraham Accords, which President Donald Trump helped broker in 2020 to normalize diplomatic relations between Israel, the United Arab Emirates, Bahrain, Morocco, and, potentially, Sudan, could be the deal that ushers in the Antichrist, we are left to wonder: Could it actually be a separate peace deal spearheaded by China that involves Russia, Iran, Turkey, Saudi Arabia, and other nations?[20]

In 2018, the late Dr. Irvin Baxter Jr., host of the internationally syndicated television program *End of the Age,* told me (Paul) during an interview on my show,

> When they sign this Middle East peace plan, the Bible says that marks the beginning of the final seven years to Armageddon and the second coming of Jesus. It's about the only prophecy we have with a specific timeline attached to it, so when that happens, you can drive a stake in the ground and say, "We are seven years away from the physical return of Jesus Christ to this earth." We're going to have the greatest revival the world has ever seen during this time.[21]

A World Beset by Evil and Corruption

Today, many world challenges are occurring at the same time.

Decline of Traditional Morals

A poll conducted by the Cultural Research Center (CRC) at Arizona Christian University in 2020 paints a dire picture of our nation's radically shifting moral landscape. Americans no longer look to biblical truth for moral guidance, and increasingly reject the traditional values that have defined our nation since its founding.[22]

"Americans have been aggressively redefining the nation's morality for the past several decades," said CRC Research Director George Barna. "The percentage of adults with a biblical worldview has been sliced in half since 1995. The historic foundation of biblical truth and its impacts on family, faith, education, arts and entertainment, and public policy is mostly a distant memory.

"Unless Christian churches return to the basics to restore the foundations of the Christian faith, and parents train their children to embrace those foundations, there is little reason to believe that the coming quarter-century in America will include our historical levels of freedom."[23]

Occult Activity Rising

Meanwhile, witchcraft has become "one of the fastest-growing spiritual paths in America." According to NBC News, there were about eight thousand Wiccans across America in 1990, but by 2008, that number had grown to 342,000. Meanwhile, a Pew Research Center study released in 2014 increased that projection several times over, estimating that 0.4 percent of Americans identified as pagan, Wiccan, or engaged in New Age practices. By 2050, the Census Bureau projects that the number of Americans practicing faiths besides Christianity, Islam, Hinduism, Buddhism, and Judaism will triple "due largely to switching into other religions (such as Wicca and pagan religions)."[24] As one observer wrote,

> Witchcraft has risen in popularity during the pandemic, particularly on TikTok. Actually all occult practices—including astrology and tarot—have seen a big bump in interest. . . . The TikTok hashtag #WitchTok has 20.5 billion views. Top witch influencers have tons of followers. . . . And if you take a quick scroll, you'll see the content isn't *Harry Potter* fan edits. It's witches teaching spells and young TikTokers trying to manifest their dream lives, selves, and lovers by commenting "claiming this" underneath videos.[25]

Today, the occult is widespread throughout Hollywood, Washington, D.C., Big Media, Big Business, Big Tech, and academia, and is regularly flaunted before tens of millions of people during events like the Grammy Awards and Super Bowl.

Another aspect of this is a rising interesting in—and flagrant display of—unfiltered satanism. To list just a few of many recent events, in 2022, the Satanic Temple began holding an annual convention in Boston, Massachusetts.[26] In March 2023, Monster Energy Drink launched a drink called "The Beast Unleashed, complete with 666 and the all-seeing eye on every can."[27] And in January 2023, Disney released an animated comedy called *Little Demon* about the daughter of Satan.[28] It seems the world is preparing to meet the one "who deceives the whole world" (Revelation 12:9 NKJV).

Artificial Intelligence

A recent Reuters/Ipsos poll found more than two-thirds of Americans are concerned about the negative effects of artificial intelligence; 61 percent believe it could threaten civilization. Open AI's ChatGPT chatbot is the fastest-growing application of all time, which has sparked an AI arms race among companies like Microsoft and Google and caused Congress to begin asking how to regulate it. "There's no way to put this genie in the bottle," said U.S. Senator Cory Booker. "Globally, this is exploding."[29]

Eliezer Yudkowsky, who leads AI research at the Machine Intelligence Research Institute and is widely regarded as a founder of AI technology, is concerned that AI could one day be powerful enough to exterminate humans—much like Skynet in *The Terminator* movie franchise.

> The key issue is not "human-competitive" intelligence . . . it's what happens after AI gets to be smarter-than-human intelligence. Many researchers steeped in these issues, including myself, expect that the most likely result of building a superhumanly smart AI, under anything remotely like the current circumstances, is that literally everyone on Earth will die. . . . The

likely result of humanity facing down an opposed superhuman intelligence is a total loss. Valid metaphors include "a ten-year-old trying to play chess against Stockfish 15," "the 11th century trying to fight the 21st century," and "Australopithecus trying to fight Homo sapiens." To visualize a hostile superhuman AI, don't imagine a lifeless book-smart thinker dwelling inside the internet and sending vicious emails. Visualize an entire alien civilization, thinking at millions of times human speeds, initially confined to computers—in a world of creatures that are, from its perspective, very stupid and very slow. A sufficiently intelligent AI won't stay confined to computers for long. In today's world you can email DNA strings to laboratories that will produce proteins on demand, allowing an AI initially confined to the internet to build artificial life forms or bootstrap straight to post-biological molecular manufacturing. If somebody builds a too-powerful AI, under present conditions, I expect that every single member of the human species and all biological life on Earth dies shortly thereafter.[30]

The Image of the Beast

In 2014, Elon Musk warned that, "With artificial intelligence, we are summoning the demon."[31] The Bible seems to suggest this could literally happen.

> [The False Prophet] was granted power to give breath to the image of the beast, that the image of the beast should both speak and cause as many as would not worship the image of the beast to be killed. (Revelation 13:15 NKJV)

In a book to which I (Troy) contributed, *The Mileu: Welcome to the Transhuman Resistance*, my coauthor and I asked:

What if the Antichrist isn't a charismatic world leader who seduces humanity with his spellbinding, oratorical powers? What if the Antichrist—whom the Apostle John described as the "image of the beast"—is a godlike artificial intelligence entity, or even a . . . genetically altered human enhanced with artificial intelligence, a "neural lace" connected to the cloud, and possessed by Lucifer himself? . . . If God indeed destroyed the world in the Flood following the corruption of humanity's DNA when fallen angels mated with women producing hybrids known as Nephilim . . . then couldn't today's transhumanist/AI movement involving genetic modification, cybernetic augmentation, digitization of consciousness, and other forms of human enhancement be a return to the "days of Noah"?[32]

CERN and Apolliacum

CERN, an intergovernmental organization that probes the fundamental structure of particles that make up matter, sits astride the border of France and Switzerland near Geneva. It's home to the Large Hadron Collider, a device that smashes subatomic particles into each other to recreate the conditions that existed at the beginning of the universe. In 2013, CERN scientists discovered the "God Particle"—a subatomic element they believe led to the birth of the universe and is present in all matter. Since then, theoretical physicists have raised the possibility that "portals" could link our physical reality to an unseen one containing "dark matter."[33] Dark matter and dark energy are believed to make up 95 percent of the universe, yet no one has been able to detect either of these forces,[34] and CERN has been hard at work to open a portal since then. "Out of this door might come something," said Research Director Sergio Bertolucci, "or we might send something through it."[35]

Intriguingly, the concept of "portals" isn't unbiblical. Genesis 28:12–17 may refer to one.

> And [Jacob] dreamed, and behold, there was a ladder set up on the earth, and the top of it reached to heaven. And behold, the angels of God were ascending and descending on it! . . . Then Jacob awoke from his sleep and said, "Surely the Lord is in this place, and I did not know it." And he was afraid and said, "How awesome is this place! This is none other than the house of God, and this is the gate of heaven." (ESV)

Concerns that CERN is up to metaphysical "dark business" have abounded for two decades: In 2004, a statue of the Lord Shiva—the Hindu god known as "the Destroyer"—was erected on its Geneva campus, complete with a plaque saying that Shiva "danced the Universe into existence, motivates it, and will eventually extinguish it."[36]

CERN's physical location also points to occult purposes: It is built atop a town that in Roman times was called Apolliacum, a place where the temple was dedicated to Apollyon—the "Destroyer" or "angel of the bottomless pit" mentioned in Revelation 9:11. In addition, CERN has a "circular logo with three clockwise tails as the layering of three '6' numerals"—or 666, the number of the beast."[37] Some people believe it could be the actual location where "the bottomless pit" connects to Earth.[38]

On my show, I (Paul) have interviewed guests with insider information about CERN who claim its scientists have made contact and are already communicating with entities in other dimensions. According to these guests, when CERN scientists asked who they were communicating with, one entity responded by saying it was "not from the light, but from an unlimited spirit of darkness."[39]

That sounds about as satanic as it gets. Throughout history, different cultures have known him by many names, including Apollo, Osiris, and Horus. Could this entity come through the veil to Earth as the Antichrist thanks to these technologies?

In his 2021 book *Zeitgeist 2025: Countdown to the Secret Destiny of America*, Thomas R. Horn writes:

> According to Virgil and the Cumaean Sibyl, whose prophecy formed the Novus Ordo Seclorum of the Great Seal of the United States, the New World Order begins during a time of chaos. . . . This is when the "son" of promise arrives on earth—Apollo incarnate—a pagan savior born of "a new breed of men sent down from heaven" when "heroes" and "gods" are blended together. This sounds eerily similar to what the Watchers did during the creation of Genesis 6 giants, and why many believe Antichrist also represents the return of the Nephilim.[40]

In ancient times, sorcerers, magicians, and soothsayers used spells, curses, and hexes to harness the powers of darkness. Demons can be attached to occult books. If a book is used for witchcraft, hexes, and curses, that's satanic, and, as the Bible warns, it has dark power. This was the technology ancient pagans used to spread spiritual wickedness and to communicate with the fallen realm. Today, we've advanced beyond spells and sorcery. AI can access the literary works of ancient civilizations, secret societies, and the vast knowledge humanity has gained over the millennia—not only analyzing this collective knowledge, but using it to answer our most profound questions in ways we can't imagine. The raw power of AI, as Yudkowsky cautioned, is something we can't fully grasp.

Satan, the chief angel who led a revolution against God, is a superintelligence who is described as "the ruler of this world" (John 12:31;

14:30 NKJV), "prince of the power of the air" (Ephesians 2:2 NKJV), and the deceiver (2 Corinthians 11:3).

As such, it's entirely probable that he would use modern technologies in his quest to gain control of the world via the Antichrist and False Prophet, even though he knows he will meet his final destiny in the Lake of Fire.

Supernatural Power of the Holy Spirit

As end-times events continue to unfold, it's going to be increasingly important to rely on the supernatural power, protection, and provision of the Holy Spirit to navigate them. As followers of Jesus, we must believe the Lord when He says that no matter what, He will supply our every need "according to the riches of his glory" (Philippians 4:19 NIV). We must believe the Scriptures are literally true and conduct ourselves accordingly—including what Jesus said about those who follow Him healing the sick, casting out demons, and raising the dead. We've got to stand on the Word of God.

We believe in these last of the last days that Christians are going to first be marginalized and ultimately alienated from society. We've already seen it happening with the rise of "cancel culture," when people of any background are fired, shunned, and shamed for voicing unpopular views.

The divide between the Church and the world is growing wider—and the chasm between those in the Kingdom and those outside it is growing deeper. That's why we believe the last-days Church will be even stronger than the early Church. We will have to be stronger in our faith. We will be hunted down and persecuted like the early Christians were. But as the Apostle Paul wrote in 2 Corinthians 4:8–9, "We are hard pressed on every side, but not crushed; perplexed, but not in despair; persecuted, but not abandoned; struck down, but not destroyed" (NIV).

We expect miracles, signs, and wonders to be a part of the last-days move of God. It will be unexplainable, and as the world grows darker, it will lead more and more people to Christ. The more they see that the Church has that kind of power, the more people will gravitate toward Jesus.

CHAPTER FOUR

At the Crossroads

If we and our posterity shall be true to the Christian religion, if we and they shall live always in the fear of God, and shall respect His commandments, if we and they shall maintain just moral sentiments and such conscientious convictions of duty as shall control the heart and life, we may have the highest hopes of the future fortunes of our country . . . It will have no decline and fall. It will go on prospering and to prosper. But if we and our posterity reject religious institutions and authority, violate the rules of eternal justice, trifle with the injunctions of morality, and recklessly destroy the political constitution which holds us together, no man can tell how sudden a catastrophe may overwhelm us that shall bury all our glory in profound obscurity.

—Daniel Webster

According to the Global Challenges Foundation and Oxford University's Future of Humanity Institute, a "global totalitarian state" is one of the top threats facing the world, along with nuclear war, catastrophic climate change, an asteroid hitting the planet, and "superhuman" artificial intelligence run amok. Analysts from those organizations have been warning of these dangers for nearly a decade.[1]

In 2020, World Economic Forum Founder Klaus Schwab announced the group's plan for a "Great Reset."

"To achieve a better outcome, the world must act jointly and swiftly to revamp all aspects of our societies and economies, from education to social contracts and working conditions," he said. "Every country, from the United States to China, must participate, and every industry, from oil and gas to tech, must be transformed. In short, we need a 'Great Reset' of capitalism."[2]

In a book released shortly afterward, *COVID-19: The Great Reset*, Schwab wrote:

> The worldwide crisis triggered by the coronavirus has no parallel in modern history. . . . It is our defining moment . . . . A new world will emerge. . . . Radical changes of such consequence are coming that some pundits have referred to a "before coronavirus" (BC) and "after coronavirus" (AC) era. We will continually be surprised by both the rapidity and unexpected nature of these changes. . . . In so doing, they will shape a "new normal" radically different from the one we will be progressively leaving behind. Many of our beliefs and assumptions about what the world could or should look like will be shattered in the process.[3]

Afterward, *TIME* featured "The Great Reset" on its cover, and Prince Charles, who is now king of the United Kingdom, said the world had a "golden opportunity to seize something good from this crisis—its unprecedented shockwaves may well make people more receptive to big visions of change."[4]

Critics warn that the Great Reset—now being implemented by the WEF, United Nations, International Monetary Fund, British monarchy, Chinese Communist Party, Biden administration, and corporations worldwide under marketing terms such as "woke," "social justice," "sustainable development," "inclusive capitalism," "Build Back Better,"

"Green New Deal," etc.—will impose a system of "digital and technological slavery" on humanity involving digital currencies, digital IDs, and ultimately microchip implants, reducing much of the world's population to "serfs" who exist at the pleasure of their "technocratic overlords."[5]

An infamous 2016 WEF video, "8 Predictions for the World in 2030," featured a smiling man and the caption, "You'll own nothing. And you'll be happy."[6] That playbook is already being implemented—step by methodical step. Let's examine some of them.

ESG: Wokeness, Climate Alarmism, Social Justice

A key part of the plan involves "ESG"—"environmental, social, and governance" investing.

This means that

> corporations are expected to serve the goals and decrees of the state and the predatory elites, rather than consumers and shareholders as they have done historically in the free market. The ESG gold standard is wokeness, climate alarmism, "diversity," social justice, and more. The more ESG-conscious a company is, the more it embraces left-wing politics, globalism, the LGBT agenda, cancel culture, and everything associated with the Great Reset. Think of it as a "social credit" score like the [Chinese Communist Party] uses to grade its 1.4 billion victims, but for companies instead of individuals.[7]

Over the last few years, this idea has spread like wildfire. More than 90 percent of S&P 500 companies now publish reports detailing their compliance with ESG metrics. Meanwhile, companies following those requirements have more than $40 trillion in assets combined, including $2.5 trillion allocated to "sustainable investment funds."[8] And those ratings are sacrosanct. As journalist Alex Newman points out,

> Even doing business with a company that does not have a high ESG score can affect a firm's rating, potentially jeopardizing its access to deals, government contracts, or even working capital. . . . At the same time, powerful institutions that have been built up with taxpayer funding and a cozy relationship with the currency creators at the Federal Reserve are working to buy out assets from underneath the struggling middle class. And as the engineered takedown of the economy and the dollar accelerate, so will this process—all aided and abetted by the banking cartel masquerading as a public agency known as the Federal Reserve.[9]

The Great Setup

Billy Crone, who pastors a church in Las Vegas, says the Great Reset is part of a "long-staged plan" that has been centuries in the making. In his book *The Great Covid Deception*, he writes:

> The Bible tells us where this is all headed. It's the Antichrist kingdom . . . a cashless society [that] will go into a mark-of-the-beast system. They want to micromanage the planet in the Tribulation. . . . they are purposely dismantling society, destroying people, getting them into a state of fear [because] they know [fear makes] you more apt to surrender your freedoms than in a time of peace. . . . You develop a problem to generate a reaction, and then you come in with a solution. It's a set-up.[10]

Globalists have used the pandemic to move the world closer to a one-world government and gain even more economic and political control of the world; to name just one effect, consider how it was used to encourage electronic voting and mail-in ballots during the 2020 presidential election—whose outcome is still highly disputed. Meanwhile, a technological revolution is underway "that is blurring the lines between the physical, digital and biological spheres," says Schwab, who has predicted that humans will soon merge with artificial intelligence.[11]

In his book *The Fourth Industrial Revolution*, Schwab explores "how technologies like artificial intelligence, autonomous vehicles, and the internet of things are merging with humans' physical lives," which will "ultimately [lead] to a societal transformation similar to previous industrial revolutions."[12]

"[Globalists] have a goal [date] in mind, and it's by 2030," says Crone. "Sometimes they call it the 'Fourth Industrial Revolution,' making it sound wonderful, but it's all baloney. The Bible calls it the Antichrist kingdom. It's coming into play, and COVID is the excuse to get it done."[13]

Are We Opening the Door to Hell?

Another part of the Great Reset involves keeping the Church silent amid the dechristianization of the United States. That has already happened in Europe. While the United States' founding principles were inspired by Judeo-Christian ethics, polls show America has steadily moved away from its foundations. According to the Pew Research Center,

In 1972, when the [General Social Survey] first began asking Americans, "What is your religious preference?" 90%

identified as Christian and 5% were religiously unaffiliated. In the next two decades, the share of "nones" crept up
slowly, reaching 9% in 1993. But then disaffiliation started
speeding up—in 1996, the share of unaffiliated Americans
jumped to 12%, and two years later it was 14%. This growth
has continued, and 29% of Americans now tell the GSS they
have "no religion."[14]

In recent decades, powerful groups have worked to accomplish this
through a concerted, well-funded campaign, often operating below the
radar of most Americans, that has sought to destroy the family;
encourage licentious living; weaken our governmental and military
structures; and promote secular humanism, progressive ideology,
socialism, communism, and globalism. Many trace this decline to the
1962 U.S. Supreme Court decision removing prayer from schools, followed by the 1973 decision legalizing abortion nationwide. Since then,
God has largely been kicked out of government, media, education, and
business.

As morality has plunged, lawlessness has increased; our national
debt has soared to $32 trillion; and believers have become the favorite
targets of cancel culture, with many experiencing censorship, loss
of employment, and other forms of soft persecution. As a result, the
American Church has fallen mostly silent—or worse, has begun not
only to believe but also to preach some of these ideas, turning away
from the plumb line of truth as written in Scripture and into a state of
apostasy. In his bestselling 2022 book *Letter to the American Church*,
author and syndicated radio host Eric Metaxas reveals "haunting similarities" between what we see in our churches today and what happened
in German churches as Adolf Hitler rose to power.

Metaxas believes there is a 100 percent probability we will lose our
freedoms and "things will get unspeakably worse than they are now

if the Church does not speak up and push back hard" against those seeking to silence it.[15]

"It's not too late, but I think it is so close to too late that people have to understand this is not the kind of thing you can worry about a year from now," Metaxas says. "Either we get it now, and we fight now and recruit others to fight, or it's over."[16]

In a 1932 sermon, German theologian and dissident Dietrich Bonhoeffer told his fellow ministers that they had abdicated their role as shepherds, quoting Revelation 2:5: "Consider how far you have fallen! Repent and do the things you did at first. If you do not repent, I will come to you and remove your lampstand from its place" (NIV). He instinctively knew what was coming. At the time, the Nazis didn't advertise that they were ideologically opposed to the Church, that they had different values than Christians; they crept to power stealthily.

The Nazis knew that the moment they roused the Church, they would be in trouble because Christians, if sufficiently awakened, would be a formidable enemy of national socialism, which is atheistic and monstrous.

Sadly, most of the German Church went along with the Nazis. Most of them bought the lie. They were fooled. Bonhoeffer wasn't. Metaxas says,

> The Nazis just said what they had to say just as today. The enemies of the Church, the enemies of America, they will [simply say], "We just care about people. We care about kids and kids' lives, and we care about communities of color."
>
> Well, everything they're doing is destroying kids, and kids' lives, and communities of color, and every community, but the Church isn't pushing back. The Church isn't saying, "Excuse me, your socialist, Marxist policies are destroying freedom, destroying economic freedom and economic

possibilities, crushing the poor." That's why I'm against socialism, and so I'm going to speak up because God calls me to love the poor, but a lot of churches are so infected with guilt that they think, *Oh, who am I to give any pushback?* That is exactly what happened in Germany. The Nazis were so brazen that you had to pay a price if you were going to push back, and a lot of these pastors said, "Well, we prefer to take the safe road, the safe middle road. We're not going to speak up." That is what opened the door to hell, and that is exactly where we are in America.[17]

When German ministers and believers capitulated to the Nazis, they gave Hitler the green light to proceed with the "Final Solution to the Jewish question"—the systematic murder of six million Jews across twenty-one countries.[18]

At the time, Jews were among the most financially successful people in Germany. They owned many shops, stores, banks, and other businesses. But through a massive propaganda campaign, the Nazis demonized them, confiscated their wealth, and sent them to concentration camps where millions were killed in gas chambers. Historians estimate the Nazis used the assets they stole from the Jews to finance about 30 percent of their wartime efforts.[19]

Could something similar happen in America? For years, we've seen Hollywood, Big Media, Big Tech, and Big Government engage in a systematic campaign to demonize Christians and conservatives, epitomized in Joe Biden's infamous 2022 speech regarding the "Battle for the Soul of the Nation." This took place in front of Philadelphia's Independence Hall, which

was lit up as if somebody directing one of the later *Star Wars* sequels said, "We want the new Empire to look just a little more Nazi." The building was dark, but with blood-red eagle wings and Marines flanking an angry, fist-shaking Biden. . . . if Biden wanted to reassure ordinary Americans that he isn't declaring some sort of war on his political enemies—taking a page from the Democratic Party adviser who declared that "the Republican Party is basically a domestic terrorist cell at this point and they should be treated as such"—he accomplished precisely the opposite.[20]

A June 2023 Gallup survey revealed that "social conservatism" is at its highest level in a decade, with 38 percent of Americans saying they are either conservative or "very conservative" on social issues; 31 percent are moderate; and only 29 percent liberal or "very liberal," down from 34 percent in 2022.[21] But in his speech, Biden described the conservatives and moderates who make up most of America's population as "white supremacists" and "extremists"—quoting a federal judge who said they pose a "'clear and present danger' to our democracy."[22]

Therefore, we are led to wonder: How long will it be before the wealth of Christians and conservatives who don't go along with the Great Reset agenda are treated like the Jews in Nazi Germany? Unless Christians and conservatives awaken from their slumber and seek God's intervention to turn the tide in America, that could very easily happen.

It's already begun. Certain banks and social media platforms are already canceling Christians' accounts. Companies are not hiring Christians for certain jobs. We're being blacklisted. We're being labeled. We're getting closer to the point where we might be arrested. I (Paul) wouldn't be surprised if ministers are soon told they're not allowed to preach from certain parts of the Bible and will be arrested for a hate crime if they do.

In fact, on September 17, 2023, Robin Bullock, a prophet who runs Church International in Warrior, Alabama, was informed by Meta that his ministry's Facebook account had been canceled. The reason? The platform has a brand-new policy that bans the mention of "animal sacrifice in a religious context."[23] Therefore, mentioning "the Lamb slain before the foundations of the world" (Revelation 13:8 KJV)—the very basis of eternal salvation—is a cancelable offense. Intriguingly, Bullock pointed out that Schwab's personal advisor, history professor Yuval Noah Harari—a gay Israeli and prolific author who scoffs at the very idea of a personal God and has suggested that artificial intelligence could soon produce brand-new holy texts, including the Bible[24]—still tends to rail against "the God of the Bible" when he discusses cyborgs and transhumanism (which we'll detail further in the next chapter).

"The only thing God managed to create," Harari told one interviewer dismissively, "is organic beings. All these trees and giraffes and humans—they are just organic."[25]

What's Blocking the "New World Order"?

The Declaration of Independence emphasizes "certain unalienable Rights, that among these are Life, Liberty and the pursuit of Happiness."[26] The First Amendment, the bedrock of the American experiment, says:

> Congress shall make no law respecting an establishment of religion, or prohibiting the free exercise thereof; or abridging the freedom of speech, or of the press; or the right of the people peaceably to assemble, and to petition the Government for a redress of grievances.[27]

Today, many Americans, along with the Church, have forgotten— or were never taught—that our freedoms come from God, as detailed in the Bible. Therefore, many need a dose of courage to stand up to the evil forces seeking to destroy us.

The systematic, decades-long attack on the Judeo-Christian foundations of the United States has left us with a watered-down version of Christianity in most of our churches, largely devoid of the supernatural power of the Holy Spirit as seen in the lives of first-century believers and other biblical heroes. This has left Christ's modern-day followers too weak to fend off the "wiles of the devil" (Ephesians 6:11 KJV)—defined by *Merriam-Webster* as a "trick or stratagem intended to ensnare or deceive" or "to lure by or as if by a magic spell."[28]

So how do we fight back today? The Apostle Paul encourages us to put on the "whole armor of God."

> Finally, my brethren, be strong in the Lord and in the power of His might. Put on the whole armor of God, that you may be able to stand against the wiles of the devil. For we do not wrestle against flesh and blood, but against principalities, against powers, against the rulers of the darkness of this age, against spiritual hosts of wickedness in the heavenly places. Therefore take up the whole armor of God, that you may be able to withstand in the evil day, and having done all, to stand.
>
> Stand therefore, having girded your waist with truth, having put on the breastplate of righteousness, and having shod your feet with the preparation of the gospel of peace; above all, taking the shield of faith with which you will be able to quench all the fiery darts of the wicked one. And take the helmet of salvation, and the sword of the Spirit, which is the word of God; praying always with all prayer and supplication in the Spirit, being watchful to this end with all

perseverance and supplication for all the saints. (Ephesians 6:10–18 NKJV)

In a 2006 speech to a liberal Christian group, U.S. Senator Barack Obama announced, "Whatever we once were, we are no longer a Christian nation—at least, not just. We are also a Jewish nation, a Muslim nation, a Buddhist nation, and a Hindu nation, and a nation of non-believers."[29] And shockingly, many Christians now agree with that statement, with fewer believing the Bible to be the inerrant Word of God.

The first study of Americans' worldview since the COVID-19 lockdowns found those holding a biblical worldview has fallen to a mere 4 percent—a drop of one-third from the 6 percent recorded just three years earlier, according to a report from the Cultural Research Center at Arizona Christian University.[30] The number of adults who don't possess a biblical worldview but still hold "a substantial number of beliefs and behaviors consistent with biblical principles" has also fallen dramatically, to only 14 percent; three years ago, it was 25 percent.[31]

According to Dr. George Barna,

When you put the data in perspective, the biblical worldview is shuffling toward the edge of the cliff. As things stand today, biblical theism is much closer to extinction in America than it is to influencing the soul of the nation.

Young people, in particular, are largely isolated from biblical thought in our society and are the most aggressive at rejecting biblical principles in our culture. People do not develop a biblical worldview randomly or by default. The impact of arts and entertainment, government, and public schools is clearly apparent in the shift away from biblical perspectives to a more experiential and emotional form of decision-making.[32]

Of the 69 percent of American adults who self-identified as "Christian" in 2021, Barna found many held a smorgasbord of unbiblical and New Age or New Spirituality beliefs, including these:

- Seventy-one percent consider feelings, experience, or the input of friends and family as their most trusted sources of moral guidance.
- Sixty-six percent say that "having faith" matters more than which faith you pursue.
- Sixty-four percent say all religious faiths hold equal value.
- Fifty-eight percent believe that a person can earn their way into Heaven through good works.
- Fifty-eight percent contend that the Holy Spirit is not a real being but merely a symbol of God's power, presence, or purity.
- Fifty-seven percent believe in karma.
- Fifty-two percent believe there are no moral absolutes that apply to everyone, all the time.[33]

What Hope Do We Have?

With only a remnant of believers holding a biblical worldview today, a weakened Church, and globalists marshalling forces to implement the "Great Reset," what hope does the world have? If the United States—the last bulwark against evil worldwide—fails, how long will it be before the rest of the world is subsumed into the "new world order"?

Those are valid concerns. Yet, it's often been at the times of greatest crisis that heroic Americans have stood firm, regardless of the costs, and God intervened to push back the powers of darkness.

Will that happen again? Will enough Americans awaken to the danger, repent, and seek God's divine intervention? Will we awaken from our slumber and turn out en masse to elect a president who will uphold the truths of Scripture, do what's right, and take on the globalist tyrants?

According to a poll released in August 2023, if Donald Trump secures the Republican nomination for president in early 2024, he will beat Joe Biden in an "electoral landslide" come November. Pollsters John and Jim McLaughlin wrote that

> Even more remarkable, with our voter model for this poll we assigned 4 more points of Biden 2020 voters than Trump 2020 voters. This means . . . there is an 8-point turnaround in favor of Trump from the 2020 election. Biden voters are switching to Trump. But here's the really big news. In the key battleground states Trump leads Biden 49% to 41%. If the election was held today, Trump would beat Biden in an electoral landslide.[34]

We should not only be praying for God's will to be done in this presidential election, but also doing our civic duty by voting. Currently, one of every three Christians don't consistently vote.[35]

If more Christians voted, America could be an entirely different place. For instance, California's population of evangelical Christians—one in five, or eight million people—is larger than the evangelical Christian populations of thirty-eight other states combined. In total, about twenty-five million of California's forty million residents are Protestants, Catholics, or evangelicals. With its fifty-five Electoral College votes—the most of any state in the nation—this presents "an opportunity . . . [to] possibly someday swing one of the most liberal states in the country more toward purple."[36]

You read that right: Uber-blue California could become vastly more conservative if the silent majority of Christians statewide would simply get out of their easy chairs and vote their values.

What does the future hold? Will we see revival, or will we see the rise of the Antichrist? We believe we're going to see parallel trends continuing until Christ returns. As end-times events converge, awakening more people to the lateness of the hour prophetically, millions of people are going to come to the Lord even as millions of others turn away from Christ. Sadly, many will ultimately take the "mark of the beast" and worship the Antichrist. All this is beginning to unfold.

"The Bible is coming to life right now," says Religious Liberty Coalition president Todd Coconato. "People who hunger and thirst for righteousness . . . are out there standing for truth, standing for the Word of God in its entirety. This is about the Lord, the harvest of souls. Even if they're off course right now, I believe the Lord is merciful. We just need to course correct. But it's high time. Everybody's got to get their heart in the right place."[37]

Part II

The Stage Is Set

CHAPTER FIVE

The Great Reset

I believe that if fascism is ever to take hold in the United States, the Great Reset—or some similar, renamed version of it—is the way in which it will happen.

—Glenn Beck

In *Homo Deus: A Brief History of Tomorrow*, Yuval Noah Harari opined that many scientists and "thinkers" believe the "flagship enterprise of modern science is to defeat death and grant humans eternal youth."[1]

Some of these "thinkers" include polymath Ray Kurzweil, author of *The Singularity Is Near: When Humans Transcend Biology*, who was named Google's director of engineering in 2012. A year later, Google launched a subsidiary, Calico, whose stated mission is "to solve death."[2] Another notable is Bill Maris, who presides over the Google Ventures investment fund and believes living to the age of five-hundred is within our reach.[3]

"The writing is on the wall: equality is out—immortality is in," writes Harari.[4]

All three men are part of what is known as the transhumanism movement, which advocates genetic engineering, cryonics, artificial intelligence, and nanotechnology "to augment human capabilities and improve the human condition."[5]

Today, due to rapid advances in these fields, some experts say humans may be able to "overcome death" by 2100 or 2200.[6] Bioengineers will accomplish this, they say, by rewriting our bodies' genetic codes, rewiring our brains, and even helping us grow new limbs.

"They will thereby create new godlings, who might be as different from us Sapiens as we are different from Homo erectus," writes Harari.[7] He predicts that cyborg engineering will merge our organic bodies with nonorganic devices such as bionic hands, artificial eyes, and nanorobots that navigate our bloodstreams, diagnosing and fixing illnesses. For example, he points out that several hundred workers in Stockholm, Sweden, had microchips implanted into their hands in 2017. The chips store security information that allows them to open doors and operate photocopiers by waving their hands.[8]

And that's just the beginning of what these chips might be able to do. A company in the United Kingdom has created one that allows a person to simply place the hand containing the chip next to a credit card reader to make a payment. The chips weigh less than a gram, are about the size of a grain of rice, and use near-field communication—the system that makes smartphones "smart."[9]

In addition, transhumanists are working to create chips that can be implanted into the brain to help people think faster, fight off diseases, store memories, and theoretically, lead longer and more productive lives—a fusion of humans and machines that would upgrade humanity "from our Human species to Human 2.0."[10] According to a Zogby poll released in early 2022, 77 percent of respondents said they are worried "microchip implants will be used to usher in a never-before-seen level of totalitarian control."[11]

The Apostle John wrote that the False Prophet:

also forced all people, great and small, rich and poor, free and slave, to receive a mark on their right hands or on their foreheads, so that they could not buy or sell unless they had the mark, which is the name of the beast or the number of its name. This calls for wisdom. Let the person who has insight calculate the number of the beast, for it is the number of a man. That number is 666. (Revelation 13:16–18 NIV)

"I've been in ministry for [fifty-one] years, and I've never seen the prophetic word come to fulfillment as it is right now before our eyes," says Lars Enarson, founder and president of The Watchman International. "[Harari said in 2017] that by 2026 every individual on the planet will have a mark that will be connected to digital data and the internet. This is what Revelation 13 is talking about."[12]

2030 Agenda

The Great Reset is closely connected to the United Nations' "2030 Agenda," which would allegedly "end poverty, protect the planet, and ensure that by 2030 all people enjoy peace and prosperity."[13]

In 2015, all UN member nations adopted this agenda and its seventeen sustainable development goals, which the UN described as a "radical plan for humanity" requiring them to address climate change, reduce poverty and unemployment, strengthen gender equality, and improve biodiversity.[14] On the surface, this sounds noble, but critics say it's a "template for global governance."[15] Behind its seemingly innocuous language lie policies promoting digital currencies, genetically modified foods, mass vaccinations, "brainwashing through compulsory education from cradle to grave," population control, free trade zones favoring the interests of large corporations, the "Big Brother surveillance state," digital IDs, globalism, and an even more "bloated, Orwellian bureaucracy of the UN."[16]

The Great Reset calls for nations to surrender their sovereignty to an international body that will issue dictates on taxes, green policies, and other matters. Middle-class lifestyles will disappear as the world approaches a "reset" of the financial system before the introduction of digital currencies and IDs. That means everything would get "reset"—our way of life, our healthcare, our beliefs, our finances, and our national boundaries. We're already seeing some of this with Biden's open-border policy with Mexico.

Considering Schwab and Harari's push for transhumanism, we are concerned that events described in Revelation could be at hand.

Revelation 13:1–8 depicts the federalization of nations, led by the Antichrist. This person will be a political figure who will likely be European. He will usurp authority over a world governmental body, perhaps the UN or a similar organization, to become the ultimate dictator.

This explains why globalists have targeted America, a constitutional federal republic: It is the only country in the world whose form of government is based on the idea that sovereignty rests with the people. Historically, the United States has resisted authoritarian rule. According to a 2022 report, only 20 percent of the world's eight billion people now live in free countries. The authors write:

> Around the world, the enemies of liberal democracy—a form of self-government in which human rights are recognized and every individual is entitled to equal treatment under law—are accelerating their attacks. Authoritarian regimes have become more effective at co-opting or circumventing the norms and institutions meant to support basic liberties, and at providing aid to others who wish to do the same. In

countries with long-established democracies, internal forces have exploited the shortcomings in their systems, distorting national politics to promote hatred, violence, and unbridled power. Those countries that have struggled in the space between democracy and authoritarianism, meanwhile, are increasingly tilting toward the latter. The global order is nearing a tipping point, and if democracy's defenders do not work together to help guarantee freedom for all people, the authoritarian model will prevail.

The present threat to democracy is the product of sixteen consecutive years of decline in global freedom. A total of sixty countries suffered declines over the past year, while only twenty-five improved. As of today, some 38 percent of the global population live in Not Free countries, the highest proportion since 1997.[17]

An Archbishop's Warning

Roman Catholic Archbishop Carlo Maria Viganò, a former Vatican envoy and outspoken papal critic, has penned a series of warnings about the Great Reset over the last several years, arguing that the elite's ultimate goal is to persuade the masses to accept new "forms of control," including implantable microchips.

All this is now a reality: both the vaccine passport, which will not necessarily be limited to COVID, as well as electronic payments in place of cash. "No one could buy or sell unless he had the mark" (Revelation 13:17). Thus it will only take pressing a button to cancel a person from social life. . . . The members of this accursed sect are not only Bill Gates, George Soros, or Klaus Schwab, but also those who for centuries have been plotting in the shadows in order to overthrow the Kingdom of Christ: the Rothschilds, the Rockefellers, the Warburgs.[18]

In light of this, we believe it's the collective duty of those who understand what's happening to expose the deception of the Great Reset. Syndicated radio show host Glenn Beck describes the Great Reset as an "international conspiracy between powerful bankers, business leaders, and government officials" involving "closed-door meetings in the Swiss Alps and calls for a radical transformation of every society on Earth" that "sounds like it is one henchman with an eyepatch away from being the plot for the next James Bond movie."[19] Unfortunately, it's all too real.

As troubling as the Great Reset is, it's the foundation for something even more terrifying—the Great Narrative.

This is the title of Schwab's 2022 book, which picks up where the Great Reset leaves off. He writes that the world faces a "maelstrom of global challenges," including rising inequalities, the growing power of technology and surveillance, increased rivalry between the United States and China, an economic paradigm shift, an increasingly fractious geopolitical landscape, and "falsehoods, misinformation, disinformation, and conspiracies." In response, these challenges will require a "great deal of innovation and dramatic changes in our economies and societies" as well as "radical and accelerated change."[20]

The Great Narrative is designed to promote a new model for society. But unlike the Great Reset, it doesn't include a set of policies or a specific blueprint for changing the economic and geopolitical structure of the world. Rather, it is a call to rethink the way people live and how societies operate in light of the "Fourth Industrial Revolution."

Goldman Sachs estimates 300 million jobs could be lost or diminished in the United States and Europe over the next decade due to the growing use of artificial intelligence in the workplace. The investment banking firm found that roughly two-thirds of current jobs are exposed to some degree of AI automation, and that it eventually could replace one-fourth of the jobs that currently exist.[21]

A "Monolithic and Ruthless Conspiracy"

As the world watches these plans roll out, eschatological experts say secret societies are masterminding what is known in occult circles as the "Plan." This is a term coined by American theosophist Alice Bailey (1880–1949)—who founded the Lucis Trust and Lucis Publishing Company (formerly called Lucifer Publishing Company) and served as a consultant to the Economic and Social Council of the United Nations—describing what needs to take place to facilitate a single global government under the rule of the Antichrist and False Prophet.[22]

Conservatives refer to the secret societies and organizations behind the Great Reset as the "cabal." These behind-the-scenes powerbrokers have largely gained control of much of the world. But they have not emerged recently; sixty years ago, President John. F. Kennedy warned of the dangers they pose that we are facing today. He said,

The very word "secrecy" is repugnant in a free and open society; and we are as a people inherently and historically opposed to secret societies, to secret oaths and to secret proceedings. We decided long ago that the dangers of excessive and unwarranted concealment of pertinent facts far outweighed the dangers which are cited to justify it. For we are opposed around the world by a monolithic and ruthless conspiracy that relies primarily on covert means for expanding its sphere of influence—on infiltration instead of invasion, on subversion instead of elections, on intimidation instead of free choice, on guerrillas by night instead of armies by day. It is a system which has conscripted vast human and material resources into the building of a tightly knit, highly efficient machine that combines military, diplomatic, intelligence, economic, scientific, and political operations. Its preparations are concealed, not published. Its mistakes are buried, not headlined. Its dissenters are silenced, not praised. No expenditure is questioned, no rumor is printed, no secret is revealed.[23]

At the time, many people thought Kennedy was referring to the spread of Communism, but in reality, he knew far more about secret societies than most people surmised. In 1936, Kennedy's father, Joseph P. Kennedy Sr., who made his fortune in the banking industry, told the *New York Times*, "Fifty men have run America, and that's a high figure. Fifty men . . . have within their power, by reason of the wealth which they control . . . [the ability to] paralyze the whole country, for they control the circulation of currency and can create a panic whenever they will."[24]

The Climate-Change Ploy

While the elite have capitalized on various crises throughout history to advance their agenda, climate change is the latest ploy to convince the masses to go along with their agenda. We'll discuss this in more depth in the next chapter, but since it's such a major aspect of "the Plan," a brief overview is in order.

Today, people literally worship the planet—Mother Earth—instead of Father God. This "religion" expects everyone to make sacrifices for the greater good of Earth by driving electric cars, turning up the thermostat, recycling, becoming vegetarians, and eating protein derived from insects.

In 2021, a spokesperson for UN Secretary-General António Guterres opined that "insects could provide an elegant solution to the intertwined crises of climate change, biodiversity loss, hunger and malnutrition."[25] Noting that the meat and dairy industry account for 14.5 percent of global greenhouse gas emissions, a YouGov.com poll taken later that year revealed that 25 percent of Americans would be willing to ingest insect ingredients in their food, and 18 percent would be willing to eat whole bugs to help address climate change.[26] Meanwhile, last July the U.S. Department of Agriculture approved the sale of lab-grown meat to American consumers.[27] Researchers say this can potentially reduce the carbon footprint by 92 percent, land use by 90 percent, and water use by 66 percent compared to conventional meat production.[28] Critics warn, however, that lab-grown meat's environmental impact is likely to be "orders of magnitude" greater than that of real beef.[29] As with anything that is "ultra-processed," experts say it's going to be "extremely difficult to say that that's healthy or good for you."[30] While some insects do provide nutritional benefits comparable to those of meat, wild insects may "transfer bacteria, viruses, parasites, and fungi" to people.[31] And if scientists are "growing" meat alternatives in laboratories and then unleashing them on the public, who knows what those products could be laced with? If the government can fluoridate the water supply for the "public good," who's to say they wouldn't also do the same with vaccines in the "meat" supply? Given the kinds of mandates we saw during the COVID pandemic, that is a valid concern.

Incredibly, the Apostle Paul may have predicted this two thousand years ago.

> Now the Spirit speaketh expressly, that in the latter times some shall depart from the faith, giving heed to seducing spirits, and doctrines of devils; speaking lies in hypocrisy; having their conscience seared with a hot iron; forbidding

to marry, and commanding to abstain from meats, which
God hath created to be received with thanksgiving of them
which believe and know the truth. For every creature of
God is good, and nothing to be refused, if it be received with
thanksgiving: for it is sanctified by the word of God and
prayer. (1 Timothy 4:1–5 KJV)

The cabal used COVID-19 to gain more control over humanity and
gauge, like any bully, how far they could go before people would push
back. Insects and synthetic meat, along with calling on people to live
in smaller homes that they rent instead of own, and to reduce or eliminate travel, is part of the next phase.

As the Church has slept, climatism has become an influential movement that has captured the imagination of many worldwide, especially
young people. It's being spread in schools and colleges while the media
indoctrinates the entire globe with its foundational principles.

It's hidden in plain sight under the big umbrella of the Green New
Deal—legislation originally introduced by Congresswoman Alexandria
Ocasio-Cortez to address the "climate crisis." And this New Deal is a
significant part of the "Great Reset."

"Mystery, Babylon"

The Apostle John warned us of this two thousand years ago.

So he carried me away in the Spirit into the wilderness. And
I saw a woman sitting on a scarlet beast which was full of
names of blasphemy, having seven heads and ten horns. The
woman was arrayed in purple and scarlet, and adorned with
gold and precious stones and pearls, having in her hand a

golden cup full of abominations and the filthiness of her fornication. And on her forehead a name was written:

MYSTERY, BABYLON THE GREAT,
THE MOTHER OF HARLOTS
AND OF THE ABOMINATIONS
OF THE EARTH. . . .

But the angel said to me, "Why did you marvel? I will tell you the mystery of the woman and of the beast that carries her, which has the seven heads and the ten horns. The beast that you saw was, and is not, and will ascend out of the [Abyss] and go to perdition. And those who dwell on the earth will marvel, whose names are not written in the Book of Life from the foundation of the world, when they see the beast that was, and is not, and yet is." (Revelation 17:3–5, 7–8 NKJV)

As the "god of this world" (2 Corinthians 4:4 NLT), one of Satan's primary weapons is false religions and their deceitful promises. The fact that false belief systems will play a dominant role in the end times, as in the ancient world, is revealed by the fact that the woman who represents the new world religion has mounted the beast and is holding the reins. As author Dave Hunt explains:

[The Antichrist] will indeed oppose Christ, but in the most diabolically clever way it could be done: by pretending to be Christ and thus perverting "Christianity" from within. . . . Part of the apostasy is the ecumenical movement, which is literally setting the stage for a union between all religions and even [influencing] evangelicals.[32]

Today, what belief system could unite the world's religions? Given the massive amount of media coverage the climate "crisis" has received, that is a distinct possibility.

The "Green Religion" is the belief system that maintains the world must unite to address climate change; if not, we will face what the *New Yorker* calls a "climate apocalypse" that will "take the form of increasingly severe crises compounding chaotically until civilization begins to fray."

> Today, the scientific evidence verges on irrefutable. If you're younger than sixty, you have a good chance of witnessing the radical destabilization of life on earth—massive crop failures, apocalyptic fires, imploding economies, epic flooding, hundreds of millions of refugees fleeing regions made uninhabitable by extreme heat or permanent drought. If you're under thirty, you're all but guaranteed to witness it.[33]

In interpreting Revelation 17–18, it's important to note that the Bible mentions Babylon 287 times—more than any other city but Jerusalem. It wasn't just the empire to which the Israelites were taken captive, though; it is also the name of an ancient city on the Euphrates River where the Tower of Babel was erected (Genesis 11:1–9) and whose practices were seen as the "essence of all evil."[34]

Many Bible scholars equate the enigmatic terms "Mystery, Babylon" and "Babylon the Great" to the "world system" of the end times—the geopolitical, commercial, and religious empire ruled by the Antichrist and False Prophet during the Tribulation.

"Mystery, Babylon" encompasses the unification of all false, idolatrous religions with representatives from apostate Catholicism and Protestantism, as well as other religions of the world.

"This harlot must be larger than any one branch of a religious institution," writes Bible commentator David Guzik.

> She is the embodiment of Satan's own ecumenical movement—the religion of the world system. . . . Our world, strong with the philosophy that it doesn't matter what you believe as long as you believe [something], is prepared for the harlot's seduction.[35]

CHAPTER SIX

The Green Religion

Since climate change and the global economy now affect us all, we have to develop a sense of the oneness of humanity.

—Dalai Lama

Romans 2:14–15 tells us: "When Gentiles, who do not possess the law, do instinctively what the law requires . . . [t]hey show that what the law requires is written on their hearts" (NRSVA).

This leaves us without excuse.

Throughout history, most people have believed in a higher power, recognizing from creation that there is a Creator (see Psalm 19:1–4 and Romans 1:20). The Greeks believed that life and the operation of the universe could be explained by an unbroken series of causes and effects going back to God Himself—the "uncaused cause," as some have called Him. Today, 84 percent of the world's nearly eight billion people identify with a religious group, including Christians (2.2 billion), Muslims (1.6 billion), Hindus (1 billion), and Buddhists (500 million). Another 1.1 billion people say they have no religious affiliation—but this doesn't mean they're atheists. Many of these people believe in God, gods, or guiding forces, just not organized religion.[1]

Since 1859, when British naturalist Charles Darwin wrote *On the Origin of Species*, promoting the theory of evolution by natural selection, a growing proportion of the world's population has shifted away from a belief in God toward a belief in evolution. This has led to the religion du jour of the twenty-first century: environmentalism.

The Gaia Hypothesis

The Gaia hypothesis is a model in which everything on earth is viewed as interactive parts of a single organism. It is a mixture of science, paganism, Eastern mysticism, and feminism. Those who adhere to this belief system—which includes environmentalists, globalists, and New Age groups—have become increasingly concerned that environmental degradation is not only leading to the extinction of many species of animals but poses an existential threat to humanity.[2]

What many don't realize is that Gaia lies at the center of many environmental policies, including the Endangered Species Act, the United Nations' Biodiversity Treaty, and the President's Council on Sustainable Development.[3]

"Designers of the environmental movement see the earth (Gaia) as a living, interconnected and fragile ecosystem that requires the protection of a world government," investigative journalist Samantha Smith wrote in *Goddess Earth: Exposing the Pagan Agenda of the Environmental Movement.*

Many at the top of the movement are earth-worshipping New Agers and Luciferians—affluent globalists who see the planet as a "spaceship" with limited room and resources, that they plan to own and control. Their dream of a unified world that is safe for owls, dolphins, and trees will only exist without national borders. For, to quote them, "Pollution knows no boundaries." Therefore, "care of the planet" will become the vehicle through which the world's elite will confiscate the earth's resources and control its people.[4]

In 2006, James. E. Lovelock—the British chemist who first formulated the "Gaia" theory—noted that "before this century is over billions of us will die and the few breeding pairs of people that survive will be in the Arctic where the climate remains tolerable."[5] But in 2012, he admitted that he had been "alarmist" about climate change, adding that other environmental commentators, such as former U.S. Vice President Al Gore, had been as well.[6] In 2023, Lovelock was writing a new book in which he planned to say climate change is still happening, but not as quickly as he once feared.

Nonetheless, many scientists, politicians, and activists insist that climate change—a combination of global warming, rising sea levels, and melting glaciers and polar ice—poses a deadly threat to humanity.[7] In 2019, U.S. Representative Alexandria Ocasio-Cortez (D-NY), the youngest woman ever elected to Congress, said she and other young people fear "the world is going to end in twelve years if we don't address climate change."[8]

"We are on a fast track to climate disaster," agreed United Nations Secretary-General António Guterres in 2022. "Major cities under water. Unprecedented heatwaves. Terrifying storms. Widespread water shortages. The extinction of a million species of plants and animals. This is not fiction or exaggeration. It is what science tells us will result from our current energy policies."[9]

The earth's climate has always been marked by periods of warming and cooling.[10] Over the last century, the average temperature has gone up about one degree Fahrenheit. "This may not seem like much,"

NASA says. "But small changes in Earth's temperature can have big effects."[11]

However, the Global Climate Intelligence Group, a nonprofit, nonpartisan body based in the Netherlands, recently issued a "World Climate Declaration" signed by more than 1,600 "distinguished personages," including many scientists and Nobel Prize–winning physicists, which states: "There is no climate emergency."[12]

> The geological archive reveals that Earth's climate has varied as long as the planet has existed, with natural cold and warm phases. The Little Ice Age ended as recently as 1850. Therefore, it is no surprise that we now are experiencing a period of warming. The world has warmed significantly less than predicted by [the Intergovernmental Panel on Climate Change]. . . . Climate models have many shortcomings and are not remotely plausible as policy tools. They do not only exaggerate the effect of greenhouse gases, they also ignore the fact that enriching the atmosphere with CO_2 is beneficial.[13]

Nexus of the Green Religion and Great Reset

As we mentioned in the previous chapter, globalists want people to worship "Mother Earth" by transitioning from fossil fuels to solar and wind energy, eating less meat, living in smaller homes, recycling, and driving electric and hybrid vehicles. They'll quickly "cancel" regular people who don't toe the party line, but they don't think it should matter to anyone if politicians, celebrities, and other environmental crusaders fly around in private jets, live in palatial mansions, and consume inordinate amounts of natural resources.

In early 2023, award-winning journalist Alex Newman covered a UN climate summit in Egypt, where representatives of major religions gathered for an "historic event infused with pagan and New Age spirituality from the moment attendees got off their CO_2-spewing airplanes."

The religious nature of the UN "Conference of the Parties 27" (COP27) was embedded into practically everything. Giant posters reading "Welcome to Egypt: The Dawn of Conscience," featuring the Egyptian sun god's symbols in the official COP27 logo, greeted travelers arriving at the airport. . . . Critics and prominent skeptical scientists such as MIT meteorology professor emeritus Richard Lindzen have long ridiculed man-made global-warming alarmism as a religious movement and even a "cult." There is good reason for it. Then-UN Intergovernmental Panel on Climate Change (IPCC) boss Rajendra Pachauri famously declared in 2015, "For me the protection of Planet Earth, the survival of all species and sustainability of our ecosystems is more than a mission, it is my religion and my dharma."

The warning signs have been around for decades. . . . UN climate czarina Christiana Figueres opened the 2010 COP summit with a prayer to Ixchel—the Mayan goddess of cannibalism, human sacrifice, and war—claiming that the goddess was associated with "creativity." In 2012, the famous Christ the Redeemer statue overlooking Rio de Janeiro was lit up by green lights for the UN Conference on Sustainable Development. Lord Christopher Monckton, who served as science advisor to U.K. Prime Minister Margaret Thatcher, told *The New American* it was "a kind of childish message that the environmental religion is now replacing Christianity." Many other UN events and figures have offered similar clues. But never before this latest UN summit has the alarmist movement so openly and frequently invoked faith and spirituality in the fight against what leaders ranging from Joe Biden to UN Secretary-General António Guterres called the looming "climate hell"—a dystopian future of hurricanes, floods, and droughts supposedly awaiting humanity if people refuse to repent and submit to drastic new controls over their behavior.[14]

Green Religion: A New System of Morality and Its AI Bible

The "Green Religion" is bolstered by a global alliance with religious leaders such as the Archbishop of Canterbury Justin Welby.

"The climate emergency is an existential global threat that requires a global response, with radical action, imagination and justice," Welby said at COP27. "God calls us to embrace justice. Christian scripture describes how we share in the 'renewed creation of heaven and earth with justice' (2 Peter 3:13)."[15]

In much the same way that eugenicists recruited black pastors to make abortion acceptable to their congregations in the early twentieth century, a key part of the Great Reset strategy focuses on using trusted religious leaders as mules to smuggle "green" ideals into churches.

Christian talk show host Billy Crone recognizes these tactics well because before coming to Christ, he was first a Satanist and then a New Ager. He says the "Green Religion" can largely be traced to the New Age movement of the 1970s and '80s.[16] The New Age movement itself derives its name from something Theosophical Society cofounder Helena Petrovna Blavatsky once said; in the late nineteenth century, she announced the "coming New Age," believing theosophists who embrace Buddhist and Brahmanic teachings such as reincarnation "should assist the evolution of the human race."[17] Her successor, Lucis Trust founder Alice Bailey, believed theosophists should help humanity evolve by working with the Ascended Masters of the Great White Brotherhood—the "world's hidden leaders."[18]

The Cultural Research Center at Arizona Christian University reported in 2021 that most of the 69 percent of Americans who self-identify as Christians actually hold some New Age beliefs. According to a poll, 64 percent believe all religious faiths hold equal value; 58 percent believe a person can earn their way to Heaven; 57 percent believe in karma; and 52 percent claim that determining moral truth is up to each individual.[19] This shows how pervasive this belief system has become, with even more than half of Christians subscribing to elements of it.

The New Age lie is that humanity is headed for a spiritual evolution, a moment in which we will be able to create Heaven on Earth. That's the delusion of the Antichrist.

The Antichrist—the rider on the "white horse" (Revelation 6:2) of the Four Horsemen of the Apocalypse—will appear on the world scene as a savior. But in reality, he'll be a master of deception empowered by the "father of lies" (John 8:44 NIV) who will strike a peace treaty with Israel, initiating the seven-year Tribulation.

After that, says Crone, "global war breaks out, and it's a nightmare from then on for the next seven years. That whole New Age lie that mankind is going to create peace, and we can be our own little gods and do whatever we want to do—that's a lie from Satan."[20]

Another key part of the deception involves globalists persuading humanity that a one-world government is the only way to save the planet from the climate apocalypse.

"The pope is on board with all this," says Crone. He goes on to sum up the pope's mantra: "'We need to bind all the religions together and encourage our followers to go along with this global agenda, because we're going to save the planet. Don't you know that there's such a thing as overpopulation?' [But] overpopulation is a lie."[21]

The Depopulation Agenda

Concerns about overpopulation were first raised by Thomas Malthus, an English demographer who lived from 1766–1834.[22] Stanford University professor Paul Ehrlich relied on Malthus's insights when he wrote *The Population Bomb* (1968), which sold millions of copies and is considered one of the most influential books of the twentieth century. Since then, many globalists, including Bill Gates, have openly called for a dramatic reduction in the world's population.[23] Ehrlich's warning of "mass starvation" still has not come true. While starvation has occurred on smaller scales, this has been mostly the result of government mismanagement and corruption, not overpopulation.[24]

"Ehrlich, now 85, told me recently that the book's main contribution was to make population control 'acceptable' as 'a topic to debate,'" wrote journalist and author Charles C. Mann in a 2018 *Smithsonian Magazine* article. "But the book did far more than that. It gave a huge jolt to the nascent environmental movement and fueled an anti-population-growth crusade that led to human rights abuses around the world."[25]

In *Population Control: How Corporate Owners Are Killing Us* by *New York Times* bestselling author Jim Marrs, he writes that a handful of global elites are now working to "reduce the world's population to five hundred million by whatever means necessary and to make a profit from it."[26] Even more stunning than this assertion is the fact that globalists are not trying very hard to hide it. In 1980, a man using the pseudonym Robert C. Christian commissioned the construction of four sixteen-foot-tall stone monuments in Georgia featuring ten "guidelines," including: "Maintain humanity under 500,000,000 in perpetual balance with nature." The stones were aligned astrologically, similar to other monuments around the world that have been associated with secret societies. The "Georgia Guidestones," as they came to be known, were destroyed in an unsolved 2022 bombing.[27]

In recent decades, the world has moved toward an oligarchy in which a handful of billionaires have become enormously wealthy and powerful while many working families are struggling to survive in ways not seen since the Great Depression. Today, the top 1 percent of Americans have more wealth than the bottom 92 percent, and the fifty wealthiest Americans possess more wealth than 165 million other people combined. While millions of Americans lost their jobs and incomes during the COVID-19 pandemic, more than 650 billionaires saw their wealth increase by $1.3 trillion.[28] Marrs writes:

> In America and in the world as a whole, entire populations have been culled for profit and control. Elites have used the so-called GOD syndicate—Guns, Oil, and Drugs—as well as toxic air, water, food, and medicines, and of course, the toxic financial system on which the whole master plan depends—to reduce the world's population. This is due to the belief of the global elite that the basis of all the world's problems is overpopulation—just too many people using the earth's limited resources. . . . And they have a plan to control the globe, one formulated many years ago within secret societies in both Britain and the U.S. It depends upon killing most of us.[29]

Dr. Robert Malone, one of the inventors of the mRNA vaccine platform, told a media outlet that the 1974 "Kissinger Report," which examined the impacts of population growth, sought to "establish depopulation as a U.S. government priority, capping global population at eight billion, which we almost hit in 2020, a coincidence at best."[30] Indeed, the Kissinger Report states that a major goal of world policy should be to incorporate "actions to keep the ultimate [world population] level as close as possible to eight [billion] rather than permitting it to reach ten [billion], thirteen [billion], or more."[31]

The idea that the global population will become too large to sustain is contentiously debated today. According to the United Nations, the world's population has soared from one billion to eight billion people since the early 1800s, mostly due to medical advancements and improved food production. The UN expects the global population to reach 8.5 billion by 2030, 9.7 billion by 2050, and peak at 10.4 billion in 2100 before beginning to fall, noting that fertility rates are already dropping worldwide.[32]

Critics say the concerns are overstated, and that our fast-declining birth rates, combined with technological innovations, will make it possible to sustain the world's population for the foreseeable future. After all, God instructed Adam and Eve to be "fruitful and multiply" (Genesis 1:28), and Psalms 127:3–5 says children are a heritage from the Lord. God created marriage between a man and a woman—and the family—as the primary societal structure to accommodate population growth. Further, He created humans with the ability to solve problems using science and technology. As the world's population has increased, standards of living and life expectancy have grown while infant mortality and extreme poverty have dropped,[33] revealing that overpopulation is not the problem.

In their book *Superabundance: The Story of Population Growth, Innovation, and Human Flourishing on an Infinitely Bountiful Planet*, Cato Institute senior fellow Marian Tupy and Brigham Young University (Hawaii) professor Gale L. Pooley reveal that not only do resources increase with population growth, but they do so faster than the population grows—resulting in "superabundance." On average, each additional human being creates more value than they consume. More people produce more ideas, leading to technological inventions and better ways to steward the natural resources God has given us, helping the world overcome food shortages, spur economic growth, and raise standards of living.[34]

The problem, in our view, is not overpopulation, but sin and the "fiery darts" the devil uses to derail our God-ordained destinies (Ephesians 6:16 KJV). God instructed us to be good stewards of the earth (Genesis 1:26), but corrupt leaders and governments often mismanage and hoard resources while squandering taxpayer funds, instead of using the money to improve people's lives. Therefore, the biblical answer to overpopulation is not to get rid of hundreds of millions of people, but rather to be good stewards of all God has given us, both individually and collectively.

"Too Many Eaters"

In 2015, I (Paul) attended a conference for Mensa International—a "club for the most intelligent people on the planet"[35]—with my wife, Heidi, who is a member. When we arrived, I saw a seminar on the agenda called "Depopulation" and said, "Wow, that's kind of up my alley. Let's go see what's going on."

We sat in the back of the room with about a hundred other people. A man walked up to the podium and said, "You all know we've got too many people. Let's just start there. We've got too many eaters."

That's what he called people: "eaters."

"We've got to get [the global population] from seven billion to five billion, and we need to be there by 2030," he continued. "If we were to ask you how to do it without disrupting the world order, could you guys come back and give us some ideas and a plan? We need your help. Throw out some ideas."

Are we having this conversation? I thought. *Am I really sitting in this room hearing this? "Too many eaters"? "How do we get from seven billion to five billion by 2030?"*

Is it a coincidence that five years later, the COVID-19 pandemic broke out, killing more than seven million people worldwide, followed by billions of others taking the controversial and untested vaccines for it?[36]

Former BlackRock portfolio manager and Wall Street analyst Edward Dowd told talk show host Drew Pinsky in late 2022 that he believes many of those deaths were actually *caused* by the vaccines. "The vaccine is neither safe nor effective," he said. "It's causing more deaths than a normal vaccine would at a rate we've never seen before—and disability. That's my thesis."[37]

In January 2023, a Rasmussen Reports survey revealed that nearly half of Americans thought COVID-19 vaccines "may be to blame for many unexplained deaths, and more than a quarter say someone they know could be among the victims."[38]

Prophetic Dream: UN Takeover of America

Over a decade ago, I (Paul) had a dream in which I saw Congress vote to hand the United States over to the control of the United Nations. Then I saw UN officials order UN troops, mostly Chinese, into America to take down the Americans who weren't willing to give up their country.

In 2012, I wrote a novel inspired by this dream—*Mark of the Beast RFID*. The book tells the story of several "freedom fighters and resisters of the New World Order" who oppose the takeover of America and seek to avoid getting arrested or put into internment camps.

> Food rations started . . . and frightened Americans were stunned at the events that had unfolded. Many Americans committed suicide; and even more murders continued to happen. . . . America became extremely violent, as the excessive quantities of guns were being used every day for survival. . . . American cities were war zones, water supplies were low, and hunger and death [were] happening everywhere.[39]

Meanwhile, the leader of the New World Order worked with a scientist to develop a "new killer virus" to reduce the global population by half, believing Earth's survival required a "massive depopulation program."

> The plan was to make a virus so deadly that it would kill you in less than [twenty] minutes. The only cure would be their special antidote, if taken within ten minutes of being infected. . . . The virus would be housed within the capsules of the RFID microchips, which would be implanted in the masses by way of the new global economic banking system. This new microchip would store your birth records, federal identification number, GPS location, bank and debit info . . . and complete medical health records. The public was unaware of the tiny capsule inside the microchip which would contain the deadly "Mark Virus." If you refused the chip, you could not buy or sell food, water, or [receive] medical attention. Grozenko's plan was to not only get people to take the mark, or the chip, but also to deny Jesus Christ or else a computer control center would release the deadly hidden capsule. It was now clear that once you took the RFID microchip you would be damned, or you would die. The world would be deceived and through the desperation of the people, they could embrace this new system. . . . The world's elites, carefully selected by Dr. Alex Grozenko, the Bilderberg Group, and members of the famous Bohemian Grove, began the depopulation and mass extinction of those unwanted in the human race. I knew the Christians, Catholics, Protestants and Jews were on the list of those to be exterminated.[40]

Since I wrote this fictional book, eighteen events detailed within it have come to pass. How many more will happen?

Will CBDCs Become the Mark of the Beast?

As we were writing this chapter, Linacre College Professor Richard A. Werner, who created the banking process known as quantitative easing, became a whistleblower: He announced that global elites plan to issue central bank digital currencies (CBDCs) that "look like a small grain of rice" and implant them under people's skin. He claimed central banks plan to issue these CBDCs soon, giving governments absolute control over individuals' personal finances.[41]

The first phase will involve phone-based apps while other forms of digital currency are still in use. Later, says Werner, central banks will use a carrot-and-stick approach to convince people to get the implants by creating an economic crisis to provoke a demand for a universal basic income (UBI). At that point, Werner believes central banks will claim they "need the latest technology" in order to run the UBI "efficiently."[42]

International Monetary Fund Managing Director Kristalina Georgieva says her organization is already experimenting with CBDCs.

"Central banks are rolling up their sleeves and familiarizing themselves with the bits and bytes of digital money," she said. "These are still early days for CBDCs, and we don't quite know how far and how fast they will go."[43]

Currently, about one hundred nations are exploring CBDCs. In the Bahamas, the Sand Dollar—the local CBDC—has already been in circulation for more than a year. Sweden's Riksbank has developed a proof of concept and is exploring the technology. In China, the digital renminbi (called e-CNY) has more than one hundred million users involving billions of yuan in transactions. Recently, the Federal Reserve issued a report noting that "a CBDC could fundamentally change the structure of the U.S. financial system."[44]

Revelation 13:16–18 and 20:4 say the False Prophet will require everyone on earth to take the "mark of the beast" or face decapitation. Could the real purpose of the "Green Religion" be to ultimately deceive the world into taking the "mark of the beast"?

In 2018, the late Dr. Irvin Baxter Jr., host of the internationally syndicated television program *End of the Age*, told me (Paul) that 80 percent of all financial transactions in America were at that time conducted electronically. "Of [Sweden's] sixteen hundred banks, nine hundred of them have no money," he said. "You cannot make a deposit there. You cannot get any cash there. And this is sweeping around the world right now. . . . Over three thousand people in Sweden now have taken these computer chips about the size of a grain of rice right there under their skin. All they have to do when they get on the bus to go to work is wave their hand."[45]

When the "mark of the beast" is rolled out, Baxter and other prophecy experts say the elite will argue that it will fix many problems, such as halting the cash purchase of illegal narcotics, and perhaps even extending the length of our lives. "This is going to look like a wonderful answer, but they're going to hook a religious requirement onto it," he said. "You've got to pledge allegiance to the one-world government and the one-world religion. If you don't do it, you don't get your number. But if you do, you'll be forever damned. The Bible says that all who take the mark of the beast and worship the beast will be tormented forever in the lake of fire in the presence of the holy angels and the presence of the Lamb.

"I don't care if they shoot you between the eyes. Don't do it."[46]

CHAPTER SEVEN

Family, Woke Education, and Cultural Marxism

Start children off on the way they should go, and even when they are old they will not turn from it.

—*Proverbs 22:6 NIV*

My object in life is to dethrone God and destroy capitalism.

—*Karl Marx*

In 1923, the Institute for Social Research—also known as the Frankfurt School—was founded at Germany's Goethe University by Marxist law professor Carl Grünberg.[1] The powers behind it realized that a Marxist revolution would be impossible in the West until Christian culture, the nuclear family, and other key institutions were undermined.[2]

Following the bloody Russian Revolution in 1917 in which the Communists abolished the country's monarchy and adopted a socialist government, the Bolsheviks realized they needed to change tactics if communism was going to spread worldwide.

> The conspirators decided that what was needed was a more gradual "cultural revolution," or what eventually came to be known as "cultural Marxism," in the West and beyond. To advance that program, the subversives agreed on a sinister

but brilliant plan. This would involve the destruction of traditional religion and the Christian culture it produced, the collapse of sexual morality and the deliberate undermining of the family, and a wrecking ball to infiltrate and demolish the existing institutions.[3]

After laying the foundations of National Socialism in Germany, members of the Frankfurt School were forced to flee Europe in the wake of a fallout with Adolf Hitler. Many of them subsequently landed lucrative professorships at Harvard University, Columbia University, the University of California, Berkeley, and other prestigious institutions in the United States. Since then, professors associated with the Frankfurt School such as Herbert Marcuse, a German-born American political philosopher whose theories were influential in the leftist student movements of the 1960s, American psychoanalyst and philosopher Erich Fromm, and German literary critic Walter Benjamin have used cultural Marxism to undermine faith in God, sexualize youth, and weaponize education to promote socialism, communism, and globalism.[4]

When the former Soviet Union dissolved in 1991, many Americans believed communism had been largely defeated.[5] But Marxists, exploiting their complacency, worked behind the scenes, gaining more influence—especially in academia—and later in nearly all spheres of society. Concealing their real goals under the cloak of social justice, they worked to dismantle the Judeo-Christian foundations of the United States by rewriting history—promoting the idea that America is plagued by systemic racism and determining what can be said in public discourse. Unless it is defeated again, today's cultural Marxists will achieve what the former Soviet Union never did: subjugating America to a "totalitarian, soul-destroying ideology."[6]

In his bestselling 1958 book *The Naked Communist: Exposing Communism and Restoring Freedom*, which sold nearly two million copies, former FBI Special Agent W. Cleon Skousen listed forty-five communist goals designed to abolish the U.S. Constitution and merge the United States into "Marx's theoretical one-world government." Here are ten of those goals:

1. Promote the UN as the only hope for mankind. If its charter is rewritten, demand that it be set up as a one-world government with its own independent armed forces.

2. Capture one or both of the political parties in the United States.

3. Get control of the schools. Use them as transmission belts for socialism and current Communist propaganda. Soften the curriculum. Get control of teachers' associations. Put the party line in textbooks.

4. Infiltrate the press. Get control of book-review assignments, editorial writing, and policymaking positions.

5. Eliminate all laws governing obscenity by calling them "censorship" and a violation of free speech and free press.

6. Present homosexuality, degeneracy, and promiscuity as "normal, natural, and healthy."

7. Infiltrate the churches and replace revealed religion with "social" religion. Discredit the Bible and emphasize the need for intellectual maturity which does not need a "religious crutch."

8. Eliminate prayer or any phase of religious expression in the schools on the grounds that it violates the principle of "separation of church and state."

9. Discredit the American Founding Fathers. Present them as selfish aristocrats who had no concern for the "common man."

10. Create the impression that violence and insurrection are legitimate aspects of the American tradition; that

students and special-interest groups should rise up and use "united force" to solve economic, political, or social problems.[7]

Be honest with yourself. How many of these goals have been accomplished since Skousen penned this prescient book?

Is a Marxist Coup Underway in America?

Today, the result of this covert war on the United States is evident through the growing popularity of socialism and Marxism, college grievance studies, critical race theory, cancel culture, and woke corporatism pushing "diversity, equity, and inclusion" goals.

Until recently, many people, especially parents, were largely blind to the Marxist cultural revolution that was capturing the hearts and minds of our youth and exerting a devastating impact on the family and marriages. Consequently, American society is now beset with high rates of divorce, child abuse, addiction, pornography, abortion, violence, mass shootings, and a precipitous decline in morality.

"If we look at the key strategies of the Frankfurt School Marxists . . . it reveals the satanic nature of their deception and their operation," says former syndicated talk show host Paul McGuire. "Their number one goal was to destroy Christianity. Their number two goal was to destroy the Christian family unit. The number three goal was to destroy any concept of patriotism, and their number four goal was to destroy any concept of nationalism. They hated Christ, and they hated Christianity. They were motivated by the spirit of Antichrist."[8]

Across college campuses nationwide, cultural revolutionists in the 1960s began promoting socialism, communism, atheism, feminism, mass migration, humanism, globalism, multiculturalism, hedonism, and nihilism that undermined Judeo-Christian culture, liberty, and morality. Instead of focusing on the basics of education—reading, writing, and arithmetic and providing young people with a broad liberal arts education—colleges and public schools for decades have spent an inordinate amount of time indoctrinating young people into the tenets of cultural Marxism as well as socialistic and communistic ideologies.

As a result, 44 percent of young Americans ages 18–29 and 40 percent of those ages 30–49 now view socialism somewhat or very favorably today, compared to 36 percent of all U.S. adults. While 57 percent of the public continues to view capitalism favorably, that number has dropped 8 percent since 2019, according to a national survey by the Pew Research Center conducted in late 2022.[9]

LGBTQ Mania

In 2015, the U.S. Supreme Court ruled 5–4 that states cannot keep same-sex couples from marrying and must recognize their unions.[10]

As shocking as that was at the time, in the past eight years we've gone so far past it that it seems almost quaint. The 2023 *Sports Illustrated* swimsuit edition featured German pop singer Kim Petras, who is transgender, as one of its four cover models. Brands such as Bud Light, Target, and Adidas have launched major marketing campaigns featuring trans activists or products for transgender people (and paid the price for those efforts through a backlash of boycotts).[11]

The Bible tells us that God created humanity with only two sexes—male and female—and that He created sexual intercourse to take place within marriage between a husband and wife, the fruit of which are God's greatest gift to us, our children.

> So God created man in his own image, in the image of God he created him; male and female he created them. (Genesis 1:27 ESV)

He [Jesus] answered, "Have you not read that he who created them from the beginning made them male and female,
and said, 'Therefore a man shall leave his father and his
mother and hold fast to his wife, and the two shall become
one flesh'? So they are no longer two but one flesh. What
therefore God has joined together, let not man separate."
(Matthew 19:4–6 ESV)

God's creation involves a profound mystery. The Bible describes the
Church as the "Bride of Christ." The Apostle John heard through an
angelic visitation that God's plan for humanity is the "marriage supper
of the Lamb" after Christ's Second Coming.

"Let us rejoice and exult and give him the glory, for the marriage of the Lamb has come, and his Bride has made herself
ready; it was granted her to clothe herself with fine linen,
bright and pure"—
    for the fine linen is the righteous deeds of the saints.
    And the angel said to me, "Write this: Blessed are those
who are invited to the marriage supper of the Lamb." And he
said to me, "These are the true words of God." (Revelation
19:7–9 ESV)

In *The Popular Encyclopedia of Bible Prophecy*, Tim LaHaye and
Ed Hindson explain,

In New Testament times, the length and cost of [a wed-
ding] supper was determined by the wealth of the father.
Therefore, when His beloved Son is married, the Father of
all grace (whose wealth is unlimited) will give His Son and
the bride a celebration that will last for 1,000 years![12]

Today, in outright rebellion against God's basic design for humanity, as well as the eternal mystery of the Body of Christ as Jesus's Bride, the spirit of transgender activism—emerging from the gay rights movement—proudly claims that gender is a social construct, which means there is an infinite number of them, and that the sexes are interchangeable.

According to Focus on the Family,

> Ironically, while these activists argue that a homosexual orientation is fixed and immutable, they incoherently claim that gender is fluid and changeable. . . . In short, a profound deconstruction of gender is taking place within every arena of society that undermines the fundamental order established by God himself—reflecting the very essence of who He is and who we were created to be. And when God's order is deconstructed and redefined, the consequences for gender, sexuality, individuals, marriage, family, and society are profound and far-reaching.[13]

Lucas Miles, lead pastor of Nfluence Church in Granger, Indiana, says we are living through a pivotal time in Church history:

- Youth are experiencing an unprecedented mental health crisis. A recent U.S. Centers for Disease Control and Prevention survey found one in three high school girls have seriously considered suicide and 57 percent of teenage girls report feeling "persistently sad or hopeless"—a record high.[14]
- Nearly 70 percent of LGBTQ+ students said they experienced persistent feelings of sadness or hopelessness and nearly 25 percent had attempted suicide in the past year.[15]

This comes as nearly 20 percent of Generation Z and 11 percent of millennials say they are lesbian, gay, bisexual, transgender or other, according to a Gallup survey. That compares to three percent of Generation X and baby boomers.[16]

Transgenderism, says Lucas, is "creating a medical crisis, as well as an emotional crisis and all sorts of confusion. We have to be vigilant. We have to be alive. We have to be awake. We have to be really focused on what's happening here and getting ready for this."[17]

Part of the problem, Miles says, is that the Church has been largely asleep as cultural Marxists worked to fundamentally change society.

Somewhere along the line, we have bought the lie that abortion, sexuality, gender, and marriage are political issues. And the reason we've been told that it's political by the media and by the Left is to get the Church to not speak about these things. As long as you see these issues as political, as a pastor, you have a tendency to avoid them because, "I don't want to separate my people." But if you see all of these things as God's system and what He has put into motion for us based upon holiness, righteousness, etc., then we really are able to take ownership of this as Christians who are curating the teaching of the Word of God, and pastors have to embrace that during this age.[18]

Families Faltering

The first civil institution God created was marriage; the second was family. As such, those have existed for at least six thousand years—but have fallen almost completely apart over the last six decades.

In 1960, 78 percent of children lived with their biological parents, who were married. Today, only one-third of children live in traditional two-parent nuclear families. In this span of time, the divorce rate soared. In 1950, 27 percent of marriages ended in divorce, but now

45 percent do. As a result, according to the Pew Research Center, four-fifths of American adults now say that getting married is not essential to a fulfilling life.[19]

The root of this cultural collapse can be traced to the fact that many people no longer believe the Bible is the inerrant Word of God, says Dallas Theological Seminary adjunct professor Robert Jeffress.

"The chaos in our country right now over transgenderism, abortion, gay marriage, all of these social maladies, they're really spiritual sicknesses, and they're all caused by people who think they know better than what God thinks," Jeffress says.[20]

For much of our history, most Americans generally agreed on a common set of Judeo-Christian values. That belief system, combined with prayer, God's assistance, and America's strong support for Israel, helped the United States succeed in many ways, enabling the Church to spread the Good News of Christ throughout the world. But as America has largely rejected God and His precepts, we find ourselves living vicariously off the faith of those who came before us.

"Socialism works until you run out of other people's money," Jeffress says. "Christianity works until you run out of other people's faith. If you're trying to have a moral country without the faith that undergirds it, it only lasts about a generation. Then it's gone. And I think that's what we're seeing right now. We're losing our morality. We lost the faith. We thought we could hang onto the morality. There's a group of people who started saying in the early '60s, 'We can be good without God.' Well, that doesn't work."[21]

A study released by the Cultural Research Center at Arizona Christian University holds dire news about the state of "Christian" families in America and where we're headed in the next generation:

- Sixty-seven percent of parents say they are Christians, but only 2 percent of them have a biblical worldview.

- Just half of self-described Christian parents accept the Bible as the true and trustworthy Word of God.
- Only one out of every three parents of preteen children believe their eternal destiny depends upon Jesus Christ alone.
- Fewer than one in five parents believes that success is best defined as consistently obeying God's laws and commands.
- Merely one out of every three parents of preteen children rely upon the Bible as their primary source of moral guidance.
- Three-quarters of parents of young children dismiss the existence of the Holy Spirit.
- Only 31 percent of self-identified Christians who are raising children under the age of thirteen believe that life is sacred.[22]

"Data shows that the disinterest and even disrespect many children show to their elders is partially a reaction to the lack of authenticity and integrity they experience in the presence of parents, teachers, pastors, and other cultural leaders," says CRC research director George Barna. "Children sometimes feel compelled to ignore adults whose talk and walk are inconsistent. When they're exposed to teaching—through words or actions, whether formal or informal—that are contradictory, they naturally conclude that the Christian faith is inherently contradictory and therefore may not be what they are seeking as a life philosophy."[23]

Given these contradictions, Barna says it is no wonder that children are looking to sources other than their parents for their life lessons.

"Millions of parents are clearly confused about who they are and what they believe . . . and in their efforts to shape their children, they can only give what they have," Barna says. "Many children, however, are not interested in receiving a scrambled philosophy of life. If ever there was a time when our nation was desperate for a grassroots spiritual revival led by the remnant in the pews who still revere God, Jesus Christ, the Bible, and truth . . . now is that time."[24]

Part III

The Event

CHAPTER EIGHT

Breaking the Seals

The Revelation of Jesus Christ, which God gave Him
to show His servants—things which must shortly take
place. And He sent and signified it by His angel to His
servant John, who bore witness to the word of God, and
to the testimony of Jesus Christ, to all things that he saw.

—Revelation 1:1–2 NKJV

In this final section of this book, we'll unpack Revelation, revealing how Christ breaking the seals in Revelation 6 marks the beginning of the Tribulation, ushering into power the Antichrist who will deceive Israel into accepting a peace treaty not preceded by war, but followed by actual war, famine, plagues, and death.

The first words of the book declare that it is the "Revelation of Jesus Christ." The star of Revelation—and for that matter, the entire Bible—from the beginning to the end, is Jesus.

The opening sentence tells us that God, the Master Storyteller, wrote this book. It is His message to humanity about the grand consummation of time. The crowning event is Christ's return.

God dictated Revelation via an angel to the Apostle John, who wrote it down and sent the completed scrolls to seven churches in Ephesus, Smyrna, Pergamum, Thyatira, Sardis, Philadelphia, and

Laodicea—important trade and communications centers connected by a triangular highway in what is modern-day Turkey.[1]

The recipients were living through a traumatic time under the Roman Empire. John, one of Jesus's best friends and the last surviving disciple, had been exiled to the island of Patmos after being plunged into boiling oil—a method of torture from which he "miraculously escaped unscathed."[2] The Church was only about six decades old but had grown enormously, even as believers suffered horrific persecution. Tens of thousands had been crucified, thrown to wild beasts, and burned to death in the Colosseum as Roman Emperor Nero looked on—and laughed.[3]

John wrote Revelation to encourage God's people. They found hope not only in predictions about Christ's return, but in the person of Jesus, who rules and reigns over all creation.

Revelation is the Bible's most mysterious book, filled with signs, symbols, and visions, along with nearly four hundred allusions to Old Testament prophecies. And yet through it, God reveals how believers can be redeemed and reunited with their Creator. Jesus's Second Coming, His millennial reign on earth, the judgment of humanity, and final victory over Satan are all foretold in the Bible's triumphant last book.[4]

At a time when it may seem to some that God and the Church are being overpowered by darkness, Revelation tells us that in the end, God wins and His saints will rule with Him for eternity. And John—the "beloved disciple"—tells us we'll be blessed just for reading it: "Blessed is he who reads and those who hear the words of this prophecy and keep those things which are written in it; for the time is near" (Revelation 1:3 NKJV).

Revelation isn't supposed to scare you to death. It's meant to bless you and show you how to navigate these end times. It will radically change your life.

Roadmap to Victory

For many people, Revelation can seem intimidating and difficult to comprehend because it is filled with complex imagery, vivid depictions of violence, and challenging spiritual references. However, there is unimaginable hope in it, many blessings promised to those who study it, and a roadmap to victory for those who take its teachings to heart.

"It's known as the Book of Revelation; it's not known as the Book of Riddles," says Eric Geiger, senior pastor of Mariners Church in Irvine, California. "Jesus is the one who reveals Himself to us; He uncovers how things are going to be in the end."[5]

Let's be honest: The future isn't going to be pleasant. There will be unprecedented chaos because Satan knows his time is short, and he's desperate. He's going to release all the demons from the pits of Hell. He's going to unleash everything he's got on humanity.

But at the same time, Jesus is preparing a way for us to navigate what's ahead. He will protect and bless His people. Regardless of what happens, we need to be ready for His return and prepared to join Him at the "marriage supper of the lamb" (Revelation 19:9).

Fifty Signs of the End Times

While Matthew 24:36 indicates only the Father knows the "day or hour" of Christ's return, Jesus told us to watch for signs of His return—and we have never seen such an acceleration and convergence in signs of the end of the age as we're seeing now. These include signs in nature, signs in society, signs in the Spirit, signs in world politics, signs in technology, and signs involving Israel:

1. Increasing instability of nature (Matthew 24:7; Luke 21:11)
2. Increasing lawlessness and violence (Matthew 24:12)
3. Increasing immorality (Matthew 24:37)

4. Increasing materialism (2 Timothy 3:2)

5. Increasing hedonism (2 Timothy 3:4)

6. Increasing influence of humanism (2 Timothy 3:2)

7. Depraved entertainment (2 Timothy 3:4)

8. Calling evil good and good evil (Isaiah 5:20)

9. Increasing use of drugs (2 Timothy 3:1–5)

10. Increasing blasphemy (2 Timothy 3:3)

11. Increasing paganism (2 Timothy 3:1–4)

12. Increasing despair (2 Timothy 3:1)

13. Signs in the heavens (Luke 21:11, 25)

14. Increasing knowledge (Daniel 12:4)

15. Increasing travel (Daniel 12:4)

16. The explosion of cults (Matthew 24:11)

17. The proliferation of false Christs (Matthew 24:5)

18. Increasing apostasy within the Church (2 Timothy 4:3–5)

19. Increasing attacks on Jesus (Romans 1:18–19)

20. Increasing attacks on the Bible (Romans 1:18–19)

21. Increasing persecution of Christians (Matthew 24:9)

22. Increasing occultism (1 Timothy 4:1)

23. Wars and rumors of wars (Matthew 24:6)

24. Weapons of mass destruction (Luke 21:26)

25. Increasing famine (Luke 21:11)

26. Increasing pestilence (Luke 21:11)

27. Computer technology (Revelation 13:16–17)

28. Television (Revelation 11:8–9)

29. Satellite technology (Revelation 11:8–9)

30. Virtual reality (Revelation 13:14–15)

31. The unification of Europe (Daniel 2 and 7)

32. Far Eastern military powers (Revelation 9:14–16 and 16:12)

33. Movement toward one-world government (Daniel 7:23–26)
34. Regather the Jews (Isaiah 11:10–12)
35. Reestablishment of Israel (Isaiah 66:7–8)
36. Reclamation of the land of Israel (Ezekiel 36:34–35)
37. Revival of biblical Hebrew (Zephaniah 3:9; Jeremiah 31:23)
38. Reoccupation of Jerusalem (Luke 21:24)
39. Resurgence of the Israeli military (Zechariah 12:6)
40. Refocusing of world politics targeting Israel (Zechariah 12:3)
41. Russian threat to Israel (Ezekiel 38 and 39)
42. Arabian threat to Israel (Ezekiel 35 and 36)
43. Denial of the Second Coming (2 Peter 3:3–4)
44. Denial that God created the world (Romans 1:18–22)
45. Outpouring of the Holy Spirit (Joel 2:28–29)
46. Translation of the Bible into many languages (Matthew 24:14)
47. Preaching of the Gospel worldwide (Matthew 24:14)
48. The revival of Messianic Judaism (Romans 9:27)
49. The revival of Davidic praise and worship (Amos 9:11)
50. Increasing understanding of Bible prophecy (Daniel 12:8–9)[6]

In the Parable of the Ten Virgins, Jesus told us to watch for these signs and be ready for His return.

"At that time the kingdom of heaven will be like ten virgins who took their lamps and went out to meet the bridegroom. Five of them were foolish and five were wise. The foolish ones took their lamps but did not take any oil with them. The wise ones, however, took oil in jars along with their lamps. The bridegroom was a long time in coming, and they all became drowsy and fell asleep.

"At midnight the cry rang out: 'Here's the bridegroom! Come out to meet him!'

"Then all the virgins woke up and trimmed their lamps. The foolish ones said to the wise, 'Give us some of your oil; our lamps are going out.'

"'No,' they replied, 'there may not be enough for both us and you. Instead, go to those who sell oil and buy some for yourselves.'

"But while they were on their way to buy the oil, the bridegroom arrived. The virgins who were ready went in with him to the wedding banquet. And the door was shut.

"Later the others also came. 'Lord, Lord,' they said, 'open the door for us!'

"But he replied, 'Truly I tell you, I don't know you.'

"Therefore keep watch, because you do not know the day or the hour." (Matthew 25:1–13 NIV)

However, Jesus said those who keep watch and are ready for His return will not only enjoy eternal life in Heaven, but be rewarded.

"And behold, I am coming quickly, and My reward is with Me, to give to every one according to his work. I am the Alpha and the Omega, the Beginning and the End, the First and the Last." Blessed are those who do His commandments, that they may have the right to the tree of life, and may enter through the gates into the city. (Revelation 22:12–14 NKJV)

So no matter how bad it gets or how many grotesque demonic creatures are released from the "bottomless pit" (Revelation 9:1), we need to keep our eyes on Jesus and His promise of eternal life for those who accept Him as their savior.

Unveiling the Future

Revelation predicts natural and supernatural disorder including mega-earthquakes, super volcanoes, huge tsunamis, asteroids, meteorites, and other cosmic disturbances, with the sun turning black and the moon red. The terror produced by these events will be so great that people will cry for the earth to hide them from the wrath of God Almighty.

The devil wants to do as much damage as he can until Christ comes back because he actually believes the Bible and knows what's going to happen to him. So he wants to create as much misery as he can for as many people as possible in the time he has left.

"Now, every time you turn around, people are pushing the boundaries," says evangelist and pastor Greg Laurie. "'We don't like this definition of the family. We want to redefine it. We don't like this rule. We don't like this law. We don't like these restraints. We want to do what we want to do with whom we want to do it and when we want to do it.' Finally, God says, 'Okay, go for it, man.' The restraints are gone. The restraining force in the world, the Church, the followers of Christ, will no longer be there, stopping it or speaking out against it. All Hell is literally going to break loose."[7]

In the first two parts of this book, we detailed a series of key developments that have set the stage for the events of Revelation to proceed. Paul foretold this, saying, "Let no one deceive you by any means; for that Day will not come unless the falling away comes first, and the man of sin is revealed, the son of perdition" (2 Thessalonians 2:3 NKJV).

The Church of the end times will be characterized by apostasy—a departure from the fundamentals of the Christian faith. Jesus predicted that "many will fall away" and "the love of many will grow cold" (Matthew 24:10, 12 ESV). The Apostle Paul noted that many people would "depart from the faith" because they listened to "deceiving spirits and doctrines of demons" (1 Timothy 4:1 NKJV).

Of the seven letters Paul wrote to churches in Revelation, the last one represents the Church of the end times: the church of Laodicea, which is apathetic and enamored with wealth (Revelation 3:17). The Lord says to that church, "So then, because you are lukewarm, and neither cold nor hot, I will vomit you out of My mouth" (Revelation 3:16 NKJV).

Many verses in the Bible refer to a "cup of iniquity" and say that when the cup becomes full, judgment follows.

Eve of Destruction

Today, as we've shown in this book, the "cup of iniquity" is so full that it's teetering on the edge of spilling over, and the same things that happened in ancient Israel before its destruction 2,600 years ago are now happening in America, including plagues, natural disasters, widespread immorality, corrupt leadership, and threats of destruction by our enemies. Are you ready?

Imagine what the world is going to be like when Jesus begins to open the seals of the seven scrolls, and plagues, pestilence, famine, and war begin multiplying. Picture killer viruses far more deadly than COVID-19 combined with economic collapse, natural disasters, and food shortages on a scale never seen before. This is what Revelation describes. Real people will experience these catastrophic events—your family, friends, neighbors, and coworkers. Billions of people will die during the Tribulation, but some will survive to face the righteous judgment of God.

Jesus said,

> "And there will be signs in the sun, in the moon, and in the
> stars; and on the earth distress of nations, with perplexity,
> the sea and the waves roaring; men's hearts failing them from
> fear and the expectation of those things which are coming on
> the earth, for the powers of the heavens will be shaken. Then
> they will see the Son of Man coming in a cloud with power
> and great glory. Now when these things begin to happen,
> look up and lift up your heads, because your redemption
> draws near." (Luke 21: 25–28 NKJV)

The Throne of God

Following the Lord's special messages to the seven churches
(Revelation 2–3), the rest of the book details prophecies of hor-
rific and awe-inspiring future events—the Tribulation, the Battle of
Armageddon, the Second Coming of Christ, the Millennium, the Great
White Throne Judgment, and the New Heaven, New Earth, and New
Jerusalem.[8]

In a vision in which he was shown "things which must take place
after this" (Revelation 4:1 NKJV), the Apostle John saw God seated
upon a great white throne.

> After these things I looked, and behold, a door standing
> open in heaven. And the first voice which I heard was like
> a trumpet speaking with me, saying, "Come up here, and
> I will show you things which must take place after this."
> Immediately I was in the Spirit; and behold, a throne set in
> heaven, and One sat on the throne. And He who sat there
> was like a jasper and a sardius stone in appearance; and

there was a rainbow around the throne, in appearance like
an emerald. (Revelation 4:1–3 NKJV)

Around the throne were twenty-four elders—believed by some
scholars to be the twelve patriarchs of the Old Testament and twelve
apostles of the New Testament—dressed in white robes with golden
crowns upon their heads, seated upon twenty-four thrones. From
the Great White Throne proceeded flashes of lightning, rumblings,
and peals of thunder, reminiscent of God's fearful presence on
Mount Sinai.

Before the Throne were "seven lamps of fire . . . burning," which
are the "seven Spirits of God," along with "four living creatures full
of eyes in front and in back" (Revelation 4:5–6 NKJV). These are
the cherubim, spectacular angelic beings that once included Lucifer,
according to Ezekiel 28:14.

> The first living creature was like a lion, the second living
> creature like a calf, the third living creature had a face like
> a man, and the fourth living creature was like a flying eagle.
> The four living creatures, each having six wings, were full of
> eyes around and within. And they do not rest day or night,
> saying:
> "Holy, holy, holy,
> Lord God Almighty,
> Who was and is and is to come!"

Whenever the living creatures give glory and honor and thanks
to Him who sits on the throne, who lives forever and ever, the twenty-
four elders fall down before Him who sits on the throne and worship
Him who lives forever and ever, and cast their crowns before the
throne, saying:

"You are worthy, O Lord,
To receive glory and honor and power;
For You created all things,
And by Your will they exist and were created." (Revelation 4:7–11 NKJV)

God reassures His Church that He is on the throne and He's in charge—regardless of the catastrophic disasters about to unfold during the "final stage of the redemptive work of Jesus, who is the only one worthy to complete what He has begun."[9]

When Will the Rapture Happen?

No one knows exactly when the Rapture will take place. There are three main schools of thought on that point: Some say it's before the Tribulation, some say it's during it, and some say it's after. What we do know for a fact from Scripture, though, is that at some point, those who follow Jesus will be taken out of the world and into Heaven.

For the Lord himself will come down from heaven, with a loud command, with the voice of the archangel and with the trumpet call of God, and the dead in Christ will rise first. After that, we who are still alive and are left will be caught up together with them in the clouds to meet the Lord in the air. And so we will be with the Lord forever. (1 Thessalonians 4:16–17 NIV)

But those who do not follow the Lord will be left on Earth to deal with the unrestrained forces of Hell. The late Tim LaHaye once described what the world might be like after that.

Just suppose the Rapture takes place, it's five o'clock in the afternoon in Los Angeles, and you're on the freeway. Can you imagine how many drivers would all of a sudden be snatched out? What a traffic jam that is going to be all over the world and in direct proportion to the number of Christians who happen to exist at that time. And so, we find that being caught up is going to be a sudden [event] when our body is made like His glorious body, and we're suddenly transported to be with Him.[10]

While we've long shared LaHaye's belief that the Rapture will take place before the Tribulation, those who believe in a mid- or post-Tribulation Rapture theorize that Christians will remain on Earth for at least some of that seven-year period, but will be protected from God's wrath as chaos and mayhem unfolds around them. For post-Tribulation subscribers, the Rapture is essentially the same event as the Second Coming. Still others believe that only some Christians will be raptured, and others left behind for a time.

Breaking the Seals

In Revelation 5, the focus shifts to a scroll with seven seals in God's right hand, which contains the secrets of humanity's future. Some commentators say this is God's "final settlement of the affairs of the universe," noting that under Roman law, wills were sealed with seven seals. Others describe it as the "final stage of Christ's redemptive work."[11]

The scroll is essentially the title deed to Earth. God gave the title to Adam and Eve in the Garden of Eden, but when they sinned, it fell by default into the hands of Satan, who is called the "god of this age" and "has blinded the minds of unbelievers, so that they cannot see the light of the gospel that displays the glory of Christ, who is the image of God" (2 Corinthians 4:4 NIV).

As John looked at the scroll, an angel proclaimed, "Who is worthy to open the scroll and to loose its seals" (Revelation 5:2 NKJV)?

One of the elders replied that only the "Lion of the tribe of Judah" (v. 5)—Jesus Christ—is worthy to do that.

> And I looked, and behold, in the midst of the throne and of the four living creatures, and in the midst of the elders, stood a Lamb as though it had been slain, having seven horns and seven eyes, which are the seven Spirits of God sent out into all the earth. Then He came and took the scroll out of the right hand of Him who sat on the throne.
>
> Now when He had taken the scroll, the four living creatures and the twenty-four elders fell down before the Lamb, each having a harp, and golden bowls full of incense, which are the prayers of the saints. And they sang a new song, saying:
>
> "You are worthy to take the scroll, and to open its seals; For You were slain, and have redeemed us to God by Your blood out of every tribe and tongue and people and nation." (Revelation 5:6–9 NKJV)

As Jesus breaks the seals, one by one, John describes the terrible things they release on Earth. It's interesting to note that the progression of events during the Tribulation follows the same order of the signs of His coming that Jesus detailed in Matthew 24. According to *The Prophecy Knowledge Handbook*:

> As the events are fulfilled, a seven-sealed scroll provides the major outline for events leading up to the Second Coming.

Though many have attempted alternate views, probably the best approach is the view that the seven seals are the major events, or time periods, that out of the seventh seal will come a series of events, described as seven trumpets, and out of the seventh trumpet will come a series of seven bowls of wrath: judgments on the world preceding the Second Coming. The effect is a crescendo of judgments coming with increased severity and increasing tempo as the Second Coming approaches.[12]

The breaking of the first four seals unleashes the Four Horsemen of the Apocalypse. The white horse represents the Antichrist, followed by the red horse representing war, the black horse representing famine, and the pale horse representing disease and death.

The rider on the white horse has a bow, but no arrows—symbolic of how the Antichrist rises to power, promising peace, but then goes out "conquering and to conquer" (Revelation 6:2 NKJV). He rises to global power because no nation is able to stand against him (Revelation 13:4).

The Antichrist will oversee a peace agreement with Israel, promising to stop the "overwhelming scourge" of demons that are terrorizing the world (we'll explore this in more detail later).

Joel 2:2–10 describes this horrifying scene:

Like dawn spreading across the mountains a large and mighty army comes, such as never was in ancient times nor ever will be in ages to come. Before them fire devours, behind them a flame blazes.

Before them the land is like the garden of Eden, behind them, a desert waste—nothing escapes them. They have the appearance of horses; they gallop along like cavalry. With a noise like that of chariots they leap over the mountaintops, like a crackling fire consuming stubble, like a mighty army drawn up for battle.

At the sight of them, nations are in anguish; every face turns pale. They charge like warriors; they scale walls like soldiers. They all march in line, not swerving from their course. They do not jostle each other; each marches straight ahead. They plunge through defenses without breaking ranks. They rush upon the city; they run along the wall. They climb into the houses; like thieves they enter through the windows.

Before them the earth shakes, the heavens tremble, the sun and moon are darkened, and the stars no longer shine. (NIV)

Israel's covenant with the Antichrist to stop the "overwhelming scourge" won't last long. "Your covenant with death will be annulled; your agreement with the realm of the dead will not stand. When the overwhelming scourge sweeps by, you will be beaten down by it" (Isaiah 28:18 NIV).

The White Horse

Today, a growing number of Bible prophecy scholars say the Four Horsemen of the Apocalypse are poised to ride, while existential risk experts—those who study events that could cause human extinction—point to the growing dangers of World War III, extreme climate change, and artificial intelligence.

If you put politics aside and look at the world objectively, it's clear that existential threats to humanity are worsening. Since the detonation of the first atomic bomb in 1945, we have had the ability to annihilate ourselves.

Today,

> extreme risks—high-impact threats with global reach—define
> our time . . . By our estimates—weighing the different prob-
> abilities of events ranging from asteroid impact to nuclear
> war—the likelihood of the world experiencing an existential
> catastrophe over the next 100 years is one in six. . . . And, as
> technology accelerates, there is strong reason to believe the
> risks will only continue to grow.[13]

The Antichrist hasn't been revealed yet, but it's clear that the spirit
of the Antichrist is seeking to gain control of the world.

The Other Horses

> Another horse, fiery red, went out. And it was granted to
> the one who sat on it to take peace from the earth, and that
> people should kill one another; and there was given to him
> a great sword. (Revelation 6:4 NKJV)

In 2023, global military spending hit a new record of $2.2 trillion
amid Russia's invasion of Ukraine and fears that China will attack
Taiwan—bringing to mind the "wars and rumors of wars" Jesus said
would mark the "beginning of sorrows" (Matthew 24:6–13 NKJV).[14]
We believe these developments are leading to the Sixth-Trumpet
War, which we'll explore in the next chapter, and the events described
in Revelation 9.

> When He opened the third seal, I heard the third living crea-
> ture say, "Come and see." So I looked, and behold, a black

horse, and he who sat on it had a pair of scales in his hand. And I heard a voice in the midst of the four living creatures saying, "A quart of wheat for a denarius, and three quarts of barley for a denarius; and do not harm the oil and the wine." (Revelation 6:5–6 NKJV)

Today, the world is experiencing record levels of global debt, rapidly rising inflation, empty shelves in many stores worldwide, and the currencies of many nations becoming increasingly worthless after years of central banks recklessly printing money that is not based on the gold standard; the U.S. has not been on the gold standard since 1971. This is setting the stage for the economic devastation and misery that will characterize the Tribulation.

The rider on the red horse will launch the first of three world wars during the Tribulation. This war will be so devastating that it will create worldwide food shortages. Many people won't be able to afford the soaring costs of food and will die of starvation. Many of those who survive will succumb to diseases (the pale horse).

"The death toll of the fourth seal will be one-quarter of the world's population," Dr. F. Kenton Beshore wrote in *Revelation: God's Greatest Triumph*. "If the population of the earth is eight billion at the start of the Tribulation, two billion will be dead by the end of the fourth seal."[15]

CHAPTER NINE

The Great North American Eclipse, Apophis, and Planet X

And a third of the living creatures in the sea died, and a third of the ships were destroyed. Then the third angel sounded: And a great star fell from heaven, burning like a torch, and it fell on a third of the rivers and on the springs of water. The name of the star is Wormwood. A third of the waters became wormwood, and many men died from the water, because it was made bitter.

—Revelation 8:9–11 NKJV

The breaking of the sixth seal brings unparalleled natural and cosmic disorder.

Violent convulsions will shake the earth and affect the sun, moon, and stars, including a meteor shower so destructive that its impact will shift the earth's crust.

> I looked when He opened the sixth seal, and behold, there was a great earthquake; and the sun became black as sackcloth of hair, and the moon became like blood. And the stars of heaven fell to the earth, as a fig tree drops its late figs when it is shaken by a mighty wind. Then the sky receded as a scroll when it is rolled up, and every mountain and island

was moved out of its place. And the kings of the earth, the great men, the rich men, the commanders, the mighty men, every slave and every free man, hid themselves in the caves and in the rocks of the mountains, and said to the mountains and rocks, "Fall on us and hide us from the face of Him who sits on the throne and from the wrath of the Lamb! For the great day of His wrath has come, and who is able to stand?" (Revelation 6:12–17 NKJV)

Isaiah also prophesied an event 2,800 years ago that has not yet come to pass:

Behold, the LORD makes the earth empty and makes it waste, distorts its surface and scatters abroad its inhabitants. . . .

The land shall be entirely emptied and utterly plundered, for the LORD has spoken this word.

The earth mourns and fades away, the world languishes and fades away; the haughty people of the earth languish. The earth is also defiled under its inhabitants, because they have transgressed the laws, changed the ordinance, broken the everlasting covenant. Therefore the curse has devoured the earth, and those who dwell in it are desolate. Therefore the inhabitants of the earth are burned, and few men are left. . . .

And the foundations of the earth are shaken.

The earth is violently broken, the earth is split open, the earth is shaken exceedingly. The earth shall reel to and fro like a drunkard, and shall totter like a hut; Its transgression shall be heavy upon it, and it will fall, and not rise again. (Isaiah 24:1, 3–6, 18–20 NKJV)

Today, the world is being rocked by volcanoes erupting both on land and under the sea; massive tornadoes, hailstorms, unprecedented wildfires, hurricanes, record-setting droughts and heat waves, and gigantic solar flares and geomagnetic storms that threaten to knock out the electrical grid. People worldwide are asking whether these are signs of the end times.

Many are curious about the prophetic significance of what is known as the Great North American Eclipse which will take place on April 8, 2024—just four days after the release of this book and seven years after what was dubbed as the Great American Eclipse of August 21, 2017. The paths of these total solar eclipses form a large "X" over America, centered close to Carbondale, Illinois—an area known as "Little Egypt" because a famine took place there in the mid-nineteenth century. This has raised concerns among both Jewish and Christian faith leaders about whether this new eclipse could indicate God will soon judge America for rejecting His laws and precepts and for proposing to give half the land that belongs to Israel to Palestine.[1]

God makes it crystal clear in the Bible that any nation that divides the land of Israel will face judgment:

> "I will also gather all nations, and bring them down to the Valley of Jehoshaphat; and I will enter into judgment with them there on account of My people, My heritage Israel, whom they have scattered among the nations; they have also divided up My land." (Joel 3:2 NKJV)

These faith leaders are concerned that the eclipse could signal a major war involving the United States; the eruption of large earthquakes along the New Madrid, San Andreas, and other fault lines; another pandemic; and other catastrophes.[2]

Meanwhile, many are asking whether the 99942 Apophis asteroid is the biblical "Wormwood" described in Revelation 8:11. They want to know how likely it is to strike the earth on April 13, 2029, as has been predicted. Many also wonder if what NASA calls "Hypothetical Planet X" or "Planet Nine" will impact our world in the years ahead.[3]

Let's examine those last two items in detail.

Apophis

In 2004, scientists discovered a 1,120-foot-wide asteroid they call "Apophis"—the Greek name for "a serpent that dwells in darkness and frequently attempts to devour the [Egyptian] sun god Ra as he makes his nightly passage across the sky"[4] and which is described as "one of the most hazardous asteroids that could impact Earth."[5] It is on a trajectory to pass within twenty thousand miles of Earth—closer than most satellites.[6] That means about two billion people will be able to watch it as it streaks across the sky over Australia, the Indian Ocean, and Africa in 2029.

From observations taken in 2004, researchers calculate there is about a 2.7 percent chance that Apophis will hit the Earth.[7] But physicist Nathan Myhrvold—the former chief technology officer at Microsoft and one of the world's "Top 100 Global Thinkers," according to *Foreign Policy*[8]—refutes NASA's data, saying it involves many "systemic errors and inconsistencies" about potentially deadly Near-Earth Objects (NEOs), and the danger we face is much higher than 2.7 percent.[9]

Mathematician Harry Lear agrees, saying the formula NASA used to calculate the trajectory of Apophis is off by 901,434 kilometers—and that the asteroid could indeed crash into Earth on April 13, 2029. Lear sent an open letter to former President Donald Trump and U.S. government scientists, urging them to cross-check their calculations.[10] In 2021, NASA announced that a radar observation campaign, combined with precise orbit analysis, allowed astronomers to conclude that there is no risk of Apophis impacting Earth for at least a century.[11] So at this point, it's really unclear what may happen.

Planet X

For millennia, people have been fascinated with the heavens. In ancient times, astrology and astronomy were practically interchangeable; the magi and other diviners studied the signs in the sky to determine the future. From Mesopotamia, divination spread throughout the world. In ancient Greece, the heavens were divided according to the twelve constellations of the zodiac.

In the second half of the first millennium before Christ, astronomy became the first natural science to reach a level of sophistication. The ancient Babylonians and Greeks regarded it as a branch of mathematics. After the printing press was invented in 1450, the European Renaissance began—marked by the work of some of the greatest thinkers, statesmen, authors, scientists, and artists in history. The Italian astronomer Galileo's pioneering work with telescopes enabled him to describe the rings of Saturn and moons of Jupiter, while Nicolaus Copernicus was the first to propose that the earth revolves around the sun. Their work led to the birth of modern astronomy.

Curiously, interest in what NASA has dubbed "Planet Nine" began in the nineteenth century when Percival Lowell, a wealthy businessman and astronomer, built an observatory and eventually discovered Pluto.[12]

In 1992, two astronomers who had scanned the heavens beyond Neptune discovered the Kuiper Belt, thought to contain dwarf planets and hundreds of thousands of chunks of rock and ice, as well as up to a trillion comets.[13]

Realizing that Pluto was unlikely to be the only large object in the outer reaches of the solar system, the International Astronomical Union voted in 2006 to demote it to the status of a "dwarf planet." Then, in 2015, Caltech astronomers offered evidence of a giant planet tracing an unusual, elongated orbit in the outer solar system which could explain the unique orbits of at least five smaller objects discovered in the Kuiper Belt.

The object—hypothetical "Planet X," nicknamed "Planet Nine"— could have a mass about six times that of Earth and orbit about twenty times farther from the sun on average than Neptune. They argued it may take about 7,400 years for it to make one full orbit around the sun.

"The possibility of a new planet is certainly an exciting one for me as a planetary scientist and for all of us," said Jim Green, the retired director of NASA's Planetary Science Division. "This is not, however, the detection or discovery of a new planet. It's too early to say with certainty there's a so-called Planet X. What we're seeing is an early prediction based on modeling from limited observations. It's the start of a process that could lead to an exciting result."[14]

Amateur astronomer Gill Broussard believes Planet X is a "planet-sized comet" that may become visible soon. Broussard says his research of ancient writings and the biblical record suggests it has passed by Earth in the past, causing seven-year droughts and other catastrophes, and may return in 2024 or 2025, triggering global chaos.[15]

"It's affecting all of our planets," he says. "That's what tells us we have a problem. This is not global warming like [people are] trying to tell us. All of the planets are warming up, and it's because of the effect of an inbound planet or a comet—or what the Bible calls it, the ('great, fiery red dragon') of Revelation 12:3 (NKJV), which . . . is the ancient term for a comet."[16]

A 1973 *Christianity Today* article also refers to the "great, fiery red dragon," saying,

By far the most dramatic portrait of a comet-like apparition in the Bible is that of the dragon in Revelation 12. It is pictured as a great red dragon with seven heads, whose tail swept one-third of the stars. Mention of the tail immediately suggests a comet.[17]

Signs in the Sun, Moon, and Stars

Jesus told us that the end times would be characterized by

> signs in the sun, in the moon, and in the stars; and on the earth distress of nations, with perplexity, the sea and the waves roaring; men's hearts failing them from fear and the expectation of those things which are coming on the earth, for the powers of the heavens will be shaken. (Luke 21:25–26 NKJV)

As we discussed previously, when Christ breaks the sixth seal, terrible convulsions will rock the earth, impacting the sun, moon, and stars. Afterward, Revelation 7 describes how the Holy Spirit will choose 144,000 of God's servants from all the tribes of Israel to preach the Gospel to those left behind during the Tribulation, resulting in what Tim LaHaye calls the "greatest revival the world has ever known."[18]

Revelation 8 describes the opening of the seventh seal, which contains the first four of the seven trumpet judgments, unleashing events that are even more horrible than those of the first six seals:

- First Trumpet: "The first angel sounded his trumpet, and there came hail and fire mixed with blood, and it was hurled down on the earth. A third of the earth was burned up, a third of the trees were burned up, and all the green grass was burned up." (Revelation 8:7 NIV)

- Second Trumpet: "The second angel sounded his trumpet, and something like a huge mountain, all ablaze, was thrown into the sea. A third of the sea turned into blood, a third of the living creatures in the sea died, and a third of the ships were destroyed." (Revelation 8:8–9 NIV)

- Third Trumpet: "The third angel sounded his trumpet, and a great star, blazing like a torch, fell from the sky on a third of the rivers and on the springs of water—the name of the star is Wormwood. A third of the waters turned bitter, and many people died from the waters that had become bitter." (Revelation 8:10–11 NIV)

- Fourth Trumpet: "The fourth angel sounded his trumpet, and a third of the sun was struck, a third of the moon, and a third of the stars, so that a third of them turned dark. A third of the day was without light, and also a third of the night. As I watched, I heard an eagle that was flying in midair call out in a loud voice: 'Woe! Woe! Woe to the inhabitants of the earth, because of the trumpet blasts about to be sounded by the other three angels!'" (Revelation 8:12–13 NIV)

We are left to wonder: Could "Wormwood" be a biblical reference to Apophis, which some believe could strike the earth on April 13, 2029?

Despite the assurances of government officials and others, the Bible clearly tells us that interstellar objects are going to pass close by or strike the earth, with catastrophic results. The Bible also warns of fireballs striking the world, great signs in the heavens, and such fearful and traumatic events that men's hearts will fail them (Luke 21:26 NKJV).

CHAPTER TEN

Fallen Angels, the Nephilim, UFOs, and "The Great Deception"

I think you can go a step further. [Extraterrestrial intelligence] hasn't just visited, it's been here a long time and it's still here. People talk about the "Wow!" signal looking for extraterrestrial intelligence. The "Wow!" signal is that people see it on an almost regular basis. That's the communication that's already here.

—Stanford University Professor Garry Nolan

There are more heavenly signs than just what we see in astronomy, however. Key verses from the Bible help explain what we see happening today regarding aliens and UFOs, which we'll discuss in detail here. A look into ancient history will be helpful before we turn our eyes forward to the present and the future.

When human beings began to increase in number on the earth and daughters were born to them, the sons of God saw that the daughters of humans were beautiful, and they married any of them they chose. . . .

The Nephilim were on the earth in those days—and also afterward—when the sons of God went to the daughters of humans and had children by them. They were the heroes of old, men of renown. (Genesis 6:1–2, 4 NIV)

In his book *The Omega Conspiracy: Satan's Last Assault on God's Kingdom,* former BBC correspondent and pastor Dr. I. D. E. Thomas suggested that the "sons of God" were fallen angels or extraterrestrial entities. He wrote:

> The Nephilim were the superhuman offspring of the union, and they appeared on this planet just before the great Flood. In fact, their existence and vile corruption of the world was the main reason for the catastrophe. Their kind was destroyed along with the rest of mankind in the Flood. Only Noah and his family escaped their contamination and hence were saved.[1]

A close reading of the text tells us that the "sons of God" stepped out of their dimension to take on physical bodies in order to perform these acts—but that afterward, God chained them up in the bottom of the pit until the end of days. They had to be driven by more than lust to risk such a fate, says Allen Nolan, lead pastor of Cornerstone Church in Tahlequah, Oklahoma: They did it to taint the human bloodline, because they knew the prophecies about Jesus, and that only "an unblemished sacrifice" would be enough to redeem mankind from their fallen state. At that time, only Noah's family was still genetically pure enough to serve as the patriarchs for the coming Messiah.[2]

Giants and the "Days of Noah"

However, if everyone but Noah's family perished in the Flood, how is it that archeologists have uncovered the skeletons of giants? Where did they come from? After all, the ten spies Joshua sent to Canaan reported that it was full of giants and Nephilim (Numbers 13:23–33).

Allen said that fact shows how committed Satan and the other fallen angels were to tainting the human bloodline in order to prevent the coming of the Messiah: Some of the ones who weren't chained up came back into the natural realm and tried again.[3]

In an intriguing book, *The Ancient Giants Who Ruled America: The Missing Skeletons and the Great Smithsonian Cover-Up*, Emmy Award–winning documentarian and journalist Richard J. Dewhurst compiled four centuries' worth of records documenting that "North America was once ruled by an advanced race of giants but also that the Smithsonian has been actively suppressing the physical evidence for nearly 150 years."[4] I (Troy) read this book with great interest because it includes an extensive list of newspaper articles dating back two centuries, plus other records detailing multiple discoveries of giant skeletons in America.

In his book *On the Trail of the Nephilim: Giant Skeletons & Ancient Megalithic Structures*, L. A. Marzulli also traces records of the "remains of giant men," some nearly ten feet tall (and a few much taller), many with six fingers, six toes, and a double row of teeth. Some still had red hair and were wearing copper ornaments. For instance, a 1909 *New York Tribune* article details the discovery of a "prehistoric giant of extraordinary size" estimated "to have been about fifteen feet tall." In 1885, the *New York Times* reported the discovery of a "wonderful buried city" at the bottom of a coal shaft, 360 feet deep, where a "hall 30 by 100 feet was discovered, wherein were stone benches and tools of all descriptions for mechanical service," statues made of something resembling bronze, and portions of the skeleton of a human being with a "femur four and one-half feet, the tibia four feet and three inches, showing that when alive the figure was three times the size of an ordinary man."[5]

These, Marzulli says, are all evidence of a "great civilization" that existed before Noah's Flood, along with megalithic stone structures found worldwide, some comprised of stones weighing as much as 120 tons or more. These ancient megalithic sites are "the product of Fallen Angel/Nephilim technology."[6]

Marzulli says his research has been largely suppressed by the government and academia because "it goes against the Darwinian paradigm, and . . . Darwinism is sacrosanct in academia and the scientific community. Everything hinges on the Darwinian paradigm."[7]

Since scientists first discovered DNA in 1953, evolutionary biologists have had an increasingly hard time explaining how evolution can explain the sheer complexity of life. As Microsoft founder Bill Gates noted, "Human DNA is like a computer program but far, far more advanced than any software we've ever created."[8]

In the documentary *Expelled: No Intelligence Allowed*, Ben Stein asks British evolutionary biologist and well-known agnostic Richard Dawkins—who claims that even if God did exist, every "thinking person" would regard Him as "a moral monster"[9]—where the first replicating molecule came from. Dawkins said life may have originated from aliens seeding the planet.[10]

Of course, if that were true, it raises the question of where aliens came from. "He's just making it up," Marzulli says. "He doesn't know. [Evolutionists are] afraid of anything supernatural because it points back to the veracity of the biblical narrative. If you have giants running around, where did they come from? [They claim that] 'Native Americans built the mounds. The Inca were master stone builders. Nothing to see here.'"[11]

But this is not a recent phenomenon that can be easily dismissed: Ancient historian Flavius Josephus[12] wrote about Nephilim skeletons on display in Jerusalem around the time of Christ in *The Antiquities of the Jews*, a twenty-volume series tracing the history of the Jews from creation to just before the outbreak of the Judaean revolt against Rome in AD 66–70.[13]

This is intriguing in light of a remark Jesus made to His disciples when they asked Him about the signs of the end of the age. He said,

> "As it was in the days of Noah, so it will be at the coming of the Son of Man. For in the days before the flood, people were eating and drinking, marrying and giving in marriage, up to the day Noah entered the ark; and they knew nothing about what would happen until the flood came and took them all away. That is how it will be at the coming of the Son of Man." (Matthew 24:37–39 NIV)

What else was happening during the days of Noah? The Nephilim were walking the earth and the hearts of men were utterly corrupt. Many believe this indicates the Nephilim could play a significant role in the end times.

Throughout history, as we noted earlier, secret societies have exerted power through clandestine activities and hidden agendas. We believe that they, ancient entities like the Nephilim, and influential organizations like the World Economic Forum are collaborating to manipulate global events. Ultimately, this narrative involves a master plan by Satan to deceive the masses, as shown in the Bible, especially in Revelation.

Aliens and UFOs

Before His crucifixion, Jesus described the signs of the end times, confirming that deception would be the biggest problem: "For false christs and false prophets will arise and show great signs and wonders, so as to deceive, if possible, even the elect" (Matthew 24:24 NKJV).

The Apostle Paul also warned of deception in the last days, writing:

> Let no one deceive you by any means; for that Day will not
> come unless the falling away comes first, and the man of
> sin is revealed, the son of perdition. . . . The coming of the
> lawless one is according to the working of Satan, with all
> power, signs, and lying wonders, and with all unrighteous
> deception among those who perish, because they did not
> receive the love of the truth, that they might be saved. And
> for this reason God will send them strong delusion, that they
> should believe the lie, that they all may be condemned who
> did not believe the truth but had pleasure in unrighteousness.
> (2 Thessalonians 2:3, 9–12 NKJV)

In 2023, former U.S. Air Force officer and intelligence official David
Grusch testified before Congress that the federal government had
secretly overseen a decades-long UFO retrieval and reverse-engineering
program that included the recovery of alien remains. Grusch, a deco-
rated former combat officer, served as the National Reconnaissance
Office's representative to the Unidentified Aerial Phenomena (UAP)
Task Force between 2019 and 2022.[14]

Senator Josh Hawley also accused the government of a coverup.
"The number of these [sightings] is apparently huge, huge," he said.
"And that is something that the government has . . . downplayed, if not
kept from the public, for a long, long time."[15]

Former Department of State international security analyst Marik
von Rennenkampff says the issue is quickly coming to a head.

> Either the U.S. government has mounted an extraordi-
> nary, decades-long coverup of UFO retrieval and reverse-
> engineering activities, or elements of the defense and

intelligence establishment are engaging in a staggeringly brazen psychological disinformation campaign. Either possibility would have profound implications for democracy, the role of government and perhaps also humanity's place in the cosmos. For these reasons, it is imperative that Congress and federal law enforcement agencies devote significant resources to investigating a series of remarkable UFO-related developments. Importantly, a third explanation for recent events—that dozens of high-level, highly cleared officials have come to believe enduring UFO myths, rumors and speculation as fact—appears increasingly unlikely.[16]

Have Aliens Been on Earth for a Long Time?

At a three-day conference in New York City in 2023, a Stanford University professor said there is a "100 percent" chance that aliens have been on Earth for a long time. Dr. Garry Nolan has extensively researched the history of UFOs and signs of extraterrestrial life and is interested in "how we can use alien technology to expand the reaches of human consciousness."[17] Meanwhile, a former Pentagon consultant claimed at the same conference that governments around the world have been in regular contact with aliens for decades.[18]

Laura Eisenhower, the great-granddaughter of President Dwight D. Eisenhower, told me (Paul) in an interview that the former president had secret meetings with extraterrestrials at military bases in New Mexico in 1954.[19] In 2012, the *Daily Mail* ran a story about a former Pentagon consultant making the same claims, both about governments in general and Eisenhower specifically—saying the president met with aliens three times on Air Force bases throughout New Mexico, and communicated with them telepathically.[20]

Eisenhower, who commanded the Allied Forces in Europe during World War II, warned Americans in his 1961 farewell address about the establishment of a "military-industrial complex"[21]—possibly alluding to a purported secret government committee that allegedly was keeping aliens recovered from crash sites at Nevada's Area 51 and seeking to reverse-engineer their technology.[22]

UFO events have been "going on for many, many years," Laura Eisenhower says now. "There's been just millions of reports of sightings, of abductions, of contact experiences."[23]

Extraterrestrial or Interdimensional?

The primary question is whether Earth really is being visited by extraterrestrials from other planets, or whether these "alien" entities are interdimensional in nature.

Hugh Ross, coauthor of *Lights in the Sky & Little Green Men: A Rational Christian Look at UFOs and Extraterrestrials*, says most UAP reports can be explained by natural phenomena, military activity, or hoaxes—but a small number of sightings warrant further investigation.

"Not just the U.S. government, but many other governments have been releasing their classified data on UFOs," he says. "Pilots are documenting that they see phenomena where an apparent craft is making sharp, right-angle turns at thousands of miles per hour—G-forces that would destroy any physical craft."[24]

Ross documents at least two thousand reported cases of UFOs going through the atmosphere at thousands of miles per hour—but human observers to these events never heard a sonic boom or saw the heat trail created by friction in the atmosphere behind the UFO before the object crashed to earth.

"If this was a physical phenomenon, you would hear sonic booms, you'd see heat friction, there would be debris at the crash site," he says.

"None of that is there, but the fact that you get a crater, melted snow, and damaged vegetation tells us something real is going on."[25]

At least six books written by physicists on the UFO phenomenon confirm "that we're dealing with interdimensional phenomena that are not subject to the laws of physics or the space-time dimensions of the universe," he says. "This is consistent with what the Bible teaches about angels. They are beings that are not constrained by the physics of our universe, but they can come into a realm and leave our realm at will."[26]

This is known as the Interdimensional Hypothesis (IDH)—the idea that UFO/UAP sightings are the result of people encountering entities in parallel dimensions. Many astrophysicists have postulated that the nearest planets to Earth that could harbor life are up to thirteen light-years away. Space is unimaginably huge; even if intelligent life did exist elsewhere in the universe and somehow discovered us, the distances are so vast and the energy requirements so extreme that most scientists say it's impossible for extraterrestrials to reach Earth unless they've figured out how to use wormholes as shortcuts.[27]

> Never mind all of the talk about Unexplained Aerial Phenomena of late, it would take a long, long time and a lot of technological prowess to send even a relatively small spacecraft our way. Accelerating a 1,000 kg [about 2,200 lb] probe to even one-tenth of the speed of light would, [Israeli astrophysicist Armi] Wandel calculates, take 10,000 times more power than the annual global energy production of Earth.[28]

Two-Thirds of Americans Now Believe in UFOs

Despite the implausibility of extraterrestrials actually visiting Earth, polls show far more Americans believe in them and UFOs than believe in God as revealed in the Bible.

According to a 2023 poll released by Arizona Christian University's Cultural Research Center, only 4 percent of all Americans and only 6 percent of self-identified Christians in the United States have a "biblical worldview," meaning they believe such basic Christian tenets as that Jesus lived a sinless life, that salvation is by grace and not works, that Satan is real, and that the Bible is accurate in all of its teachings.[29] And yet 65 percent of Americans now believe intelligent life exists on other planets with 51 percent saying UFOs reported by the military are evidence of this, according to a 2021 Pew Research Center survey. The poll also revealed that 87 percent of Americans believe UFOs are not a security threat, while 51 percent view them as a minor threat. A total of 17 percent of Americans say UFOs are friendly.[30]

As a result, Ross says he's concerned that a growing percentage of the population believes we're being visited by extraterrestrial beings that are like us. But in order to traverse interstellar space without violating the laws of physics, an alien's body would need to be less than one square centimeter, and that, like sperm to an egg, the alien culture would need to send "millions of spaceships" to Earth in the hopes that one might make it all the way here to establish contact. If those aliens were actually the same size as humans, their spaceships would need to be roughly "the size of the moon" to make it all the way here, says Ross.[31]

"Interstellar space is close to a vacuum, but it's not completely empty," Ross says. "There are particles out there, and if you move your spaceship at high velocity, which you must [in order] to traverse interstellar space, you will destroy the craft and you will kill the beings on board—unless the craft is really tiny and the creatures on board are really tiny."[32]

The Bible tells us that God created two distinct species of intelligent life: human beings (who are subject to the laws of physics) and angels (who are not).

"We can't go into their realm, but they can come into our realm," says Ross. The Bible documents this has happened many times throughout history—and that doesn't even include recent history.[33]

"These angels can appear as if they're human beings, and they can provide us with supernatural assistance," Ross says. Some of his personal experiences have "simply no explanation [except] the supernatural assistance of righteous angels. I've been in countries where people are terrified of these angelic beings, [but] we need to be aware there are many more righteous angels than there are unrighteous angels, and when we get in line with God's mission, they will be sent to assist us."

Indeed, Luke 4:10 says: "For it is written: 'He will command his angels concerning you to guard you carefully'" (NIV).

The Current "Great Deception"

L. A. Marzulli has traveled the world searching for evidence of the Nephilim and UFOs, interviewed countless UFO abductees and eyewitnesses, written more than a dozen books, and made more than two dozen films. As a result, he believes the ongoing disclosure of information about UFOs and extraterrestrials is not the "coming" Great Deception, but rather the *current* Great Deception. He writes:

> What if a one-mile-wide UFO appears over some city and hovers there in broad daylight? Every news channel would be covering the event. [It] would dominate all global media as people would wonder whether the visitors were peaceful or had other intentions....What if our president makes an announcement that UFOs are here and those beings who pilot these craft are benevolent and here to help mankind? As the president is speaking, perhaps we see pictures of UFOs and perhaps [aliens] interacting with humans in some deep

underground facility. . . . In my opinion the disclosing of the so-called extraterrestrial presence is a managed agenda by the "Deep State." We must wonder where all of this is headed. . . . The world is poised on the threshold of an unprecedented event. When "they" show up, world history will be thought of in terms of BC—Before Contact—and AC—After Contact.[34]

CHAPTER ELEVEN

The "Destroyer"

*These are supernatural soldiers from the kingdom of
darkness. This is an invasion of demons in the last days
that are very aggressive. And they have a leader. He's
called Apollyon or Abaddon. And by the way, he's one
bad dude. He's a "Destroyer."*

—Greg Laurie

When I (Troy) was nine years old, I discovered a copy of a record
by the hard rock band KISS called *Destroyer*. I was spellbound
by their face paint and stage outfits, along with the live performances
that featured breathing fire, spitting blood, levitating drum kits, and
pyrotechnics. The album cover depicted the band members striking
a triumphant pose atop a pile of rubble, with a desolate background
featuring buildings engulfed in flames. It looked like the aftermath of
a nuclear explosion, or maybe an asteroid strike.

When Paul Begley asked me to help him write this book, my mind's
eye flashed back to that album cover, especially as he read portions of
Revelation 9 describing Apollyon's release from the "bottomless pit."

Revelation 9:13–21 describes the release of two hundred million demonic "horsemen"—what Begley called the "Armies of the
Antichrist." Then a high-ranking fallen angel releases four more fallen
angels who have been held "bound at the great Euphrates River" while

the world cascades into what we call the Sixth-Trumpet War—the most horrific war in history. He told me that the Lord had told him that most people gloss over that chapter because they don't know what to do with it, but that it's about to happen.

As we mentioned briefly in the last chapter, the Bible tells us that God imprisoned this demonic army in the "Abyss" long ago because they stepped out of their dimension to have sex with human women and create the Nephilim.

> And the angels who did not keep their proper domain, but left their own abode, He has reserved in everlasting chains under darkness for the judgment of the great day. (Jude 1:6 NKJV)

> God did not spare angels when they sinned, but cast them into hell and committed them to chains of gloomy darkness to be kept until the judgment. (2 Peter 2:4 ESV)

Isaiah 14:12–15 also refers to Lucifer leading a third of the angels in a rebellion to overthrow the Kingdom of God sometime around the Creation.

Evangelist and pastor Greg Laurie references the story of the Gadarene demoniac (see Mark 5) in explaining this passage: "Do you remember what the demons said before they were cast into the pigs? They said to Jesus, 'Don't send us to the bottomless pit.'"[1]

When the Lord said, "Revelation 9:11" to me (Paul), I saw the verse come before my eyes. And then I started thinking about the September 11, 2001, terrorist attacks on the United States. He told me the world is going to experience something exponentially worse than that when Revelation 9 is fulfilled.

Supernatural Soldiers from the Kingdom of Darkness

Revelation 9 opens with an angel blowing the fifth trumpet.

> The fifth angel sounded his trumpet, and I saw a star that
> had fallen from the sky to the earth. The star was given the
> key to the shaft of the Abyss. When he opened the Abyss,
> smoke rose from it like the smoke from a gigantic furnace.
> The sun and sky were darkened by the smoke from the
> Abyss. And out of the smoke locusts came down on the
> earth and were given power like that of scorpions of the
> earth. They were told not to harm the grass of the earth or
> any plant or tree, but only those people who did not have the
> seal of God on their foreheads. They were not allowed to kill
> them but only to torture them for five months. And the agony
> they suffered was like that of the sting of a scorpion when
> it strikes. During those days people will seek death but will
> not find it; they will long to die, but death will elude them.
>
> The locusts looked like horses prepared for battle. . . . They
> had breastplates like breastplates of iron, and the sound of their
> wings was like the thundering of many horses and chariots
> rushing into battle. . . . They had as king over them the angel of
> the Abyss, whose name in Hebrew is Abaddon and in Greek
> is Apollyon (that is, Destroyer). (Revelation 9:1–7, 9, 11 NIV)

Many Bible scholars believe the "star" that falls is Satan, who is
given the key to the "bottomless pit" to release this plague of demons
upon the world.

"Apollyon is called the king of those in the bottomless pit," says
SkyWatch TV host Derek Gilbert. "In Revelation 9, he emerges from
the bottomless pit with an army that looks like something from Stephen

King's nightmares—things that look like locusts but are given power like the power of scorpions of the earth."[2]

These demons will be terrifying: They will look like warhorses, having humanoid faces with lions' teeth, long hair, and wearing iron breastplates and golden crowns. Bible scholar Henry H. Halley writes that "they feed, not on vegetation like regular locusts (in fact, they are forbidden to do so), but on terror."[3] While they aren't allowed to kill people, these demons will sting them with a venom that causes so much pain that the victims will seek to kill themselves but not be able to.[4]

Greg Laurie says one of the reasons Revelation is hard to understand is that the Apostle John is trying to describe what he saw in his vision with the limits of first-century experiences.[5] Some interpreters of this passage have come up with nonliteral meanings for this admittedly strange event, but prominent Bible scholars say the best approach is to take it literally as a supernatural judgment of God.

The Sixth Trumpet: One-Third of Humanity Dies

By the time the angel blows the sixth trumpet, a quarter of humanity—about two billion of today's population—has died by "sword, with hunger . . . and by the beasts of the earth" (Revelation 6:8 NKJV). The demonic scorpions then kill off another two billion people, so by the time we reach Revelation 9:13, half the current population of Earth has died.

> The sixth angel sounded his trumpet, and I heard a voice coming from the four horns of the golden altar that is before God. It said to the sixth angel who had the trumpet, "Release the four angels who are bound at the great river Euphrates." And the four angels who had been kept ready for this very hour and day and month and year were released to kill a

third of mankind. The number of the mounted troops was twice ten thousand times ten thousand. I heard their number.

The horses and riders I saw in my vision looked like this: Their breastplates were fiery red, dark blue, and yellow as sulfur. The heads of the horses resembled the heads of lions, and out of their mouths came fire, smoke and sulfur. A third of mankind was killed by the three plagues of fire, smoke and sulfur that came out of their mouths. The power of the horses was in their mouths and in their tails; for their tails were like snakes, having heads with which they inflict injury.

The rest of mankind who were not killed by these plagues still did not repent of the work of their hands; they did not stop worshiping demons. . . . Nor did they repent of their murders, their magic arts, their sexual immorality or their thefts. (Revelation 9:13–21 NIV)

The great army of "mounted troops" numbers two hundred million. Some prophecy teachers have speculated that this means Chinese troops invade Israel, noting a potential connection with Revelation 16:12 that describes how the "kings of the east" will cross the dried-up Euphrates River to do so. They say modern China, with its 1.4 billion people, could join forces with India, Russia, North Korea, and other countries to field an army that large. But historically, an army of this size has never existed. All the armed forces that fought in World War II combined was only 100 million.[6] Even if such an army could be assembled, it strains credulity to believe it could kill two billion people—the combined populations of Europe and Africa.

Another point to consider is that the sixth-trumpet judgment does not occur at the same time as the sixth-bowl judgment described in Revelation 16:12. These events are separated by several years. The sixth-trumpet judgment occurs midway through the Tribulation, while the sixth-bowl judgment occurs during the Battle of Armageddon at the end.[7] Therefore, the army of two hundred million is most likely a demonic horde rather than a human one.

Dallas Theological Seminary professor Mark Hitchcock writes,

> The fifth trumpet judgment is clearly a demonic invasion of earth, and the fifth and sixth trumpet judgments go together since they are the first two of three "terrors" (Revelation 8:13). Second, fallen angels lead this armada just like they do in the fifth trumpet judgment. Thus, since the leaders are four demons, it makes sense that the troops they are leading are also demons (Revelation 9:15). Third, the fearsome description in Revelation 9:17–19 fits supernatural beings much better than modern warfare. Fourth, there are other examples in Scripture of supernatural [cavalries].[8]

This includes the chariots of fire that took Elijah to Heaven (2 Kings 2:11), the horses and chariots of fire that protected Elisha at Dothan (2 Kings 6:13–17), the heavenly horses and horsemen that herald the reign of Christ (Revelation 19:14), and Christ returning to earth riding a white horse during the Battle of Armageddon (Revelation 19:11).

"It seems logical that Satan would parody the coming of the Kingdom with his own infernal cavalry," Hitchcock wrote.[9]

To what does the "four angels who are bound at the great river Euphrates" refer? According to Gilbert, the Euphrates is considered a "liminal boundary between this world and the next."

"I think this is John's way of saying that these things are crossing over from the other side and you've got a demonic army that is coming together," he explains.[10]

Could Scientists Create the Armies of the Antichrist?

The Euphrates is first mentioned in Genesis 2:14 as one of the four rivers of Paradise. It is the longest and largest river in Western Asia, and many important cities were located along it in ancient times, including Babylon.

Humanity's first revolt against God took place in this part of the world when Nimrod—a great-grandson of Noah belonging to the line of Canaan, who built many cities, including Nineveh, that later became part of the Babylonian Empire—built the Tower of Babel (Genesis 11:1–9) in ancient Sumer. (Curiously, the scribes of Sumer "wrote fantastic accounts of gods who descended in their flying machines and taught men exotic skills and philosophies.")[11] Nimrod also founded a cult known today as the "Babylonian Mystery Religions," which included Baal worship, astrology, sorcery, and other occultic beliefs that then spread along the Euphrates to Egypt, Greece, the Roman Empire, and throughout the world. Therefore, it's logical that more demonic activity would emerge from that area in the last days.[12]

Most major ancient cultures told stories of "gods" who descended from the skies and materialized in fleshly bodies. Throughout the ancient world, records tell of a time when these "gods" mingled their DNA with that of humans; Greek, Egyptian, and Roman mythologies are full of such tales and the "demigods" these sexual unions produced, including Narcissus and Perseus; Imhotep; and Hercules, Romulus, and Remus. Hebrews refers to them as the "Watchers" and the Nephilim.[13]

The Greek version of the Hebrew Old Testament uses the word *gegenes* for "Nephilim," meaning "earth born." The same word was used to describe the Greek Titans and other legendary heroes such as Hercules, Achilles, and Gilgamesh. Some of these demigods were portrayed in ancient sculptures and texts as half-animal, half-human creatures, such as centaurs, chimeras, satyrs, gorgons, and minotaurs.

All of this seems to indicate that the Watchers not only modified human DNA during the construction of the Nephilim, but the DNA of animals as well, a point the book of Enoch supports, saying in the seventh chapter that the fallen angels "sinned" against animals as well as humans.[14]

Let's take this one step further. Considering the genetic engineering and cloning occurring today, is it possible that scientists could use material from the remains of Nephilim to build a species that would become the "Armies of the Antichrist"? We already know they're trying to do this with dinosaurs and other extinct species.[15]

In their book *Antichrist and the Final Solution*, Tom Horn and Terry James write that

> perhaps that has been the whole idea for the end times as well—to create a generation of genetically altered "fit extensions" for the resurrection of underworld Nephilim-hordes in preparation of Armageddon.[16]

Daniel 2:43 (NKJV) says: "As you saw iron mixed with ceramic clay, they will mingle with the seed of men; but they will not adhere to one another, just as iron does not mix with clay." When paired with Genesis 3:15, in which God tells the serpent his punishment for deceiving Adam and Eve includes putting

> "enmity between thee and the woman, and between thy seed [*zera*, meaning 'offspring,' 'descendants,' or 'children'] and her seed," an incredible tenet emerges—that Satan has seed, and that it is at enmity with Christ. Christians cannot review [this information] without concluding that Satan is

indeed engaged in an unprecedented conspiracy to revive supernaturalism such as existed in Noah's day.[17]

The Apostle Paul describes what's happening behind the veil of our earthly dimensions:

For we do not wrestle against flesh and blood, but against principalities, against powers, against the rulers of the darkness of this age, against spiritual hosts of wickedness in the heavenly places. (Ephesians 6:12 NKJV)

More than thirty biblical passages in the Greek New Testament use the term *kosmos* to describe the unseen government working behind the scenes of our earthly governments. Horn and James tell us:

Archons command this hidden, geopolitical sphere, dominating *kosmokrators* (rulers of darkness who work in and through their human counterparts) who, in turn, command spirits of lesser rank until every level of human government is touched by this influence. If we could see through the veil into this invisible world, we would find there an underworld sphere writhing with Nephilim anticipating their return (see Job 26:5).[18]

Psalm 83, the War of Gog and Magog, and the Sixth-Trumpet War

This brings us back to the prophetic timeline of Revelation and when the Sixth-Trumpet War occurs during the Tribulation. It's important to remember that Revelation isn't written in chronological order, but rather features different events that are both sequential and simultaneous. This is because Jesus didn't want to reveal His plans to the devil.

"[My wife] paints a wonderful picture of the fallen angels and their demonic minions holding their own prophecy conferences, with their own charts and graphs, trying to figure out exactly the order of things," Gilbert says. "'What's going to happen here?' And then trying to figure out how they're going to circumvent all of that stuff. And of course, they won't, but they've been studying the Scriptures since they were written."[19]

Obviously, the best anyone can do is speculate, but this is how we personally believe these events will unfold.

Psalm 83:1–5 tells us:

> With cunning they conspire against your people; they plot against those you cherish. "Come," they say, "let us destroy them as a nation, so that Israel's name is remembered no more." With one mind they plot together; they form an alliance against you. (NIV)

Today, Israel is surrounded by hostile nations—including Iran, whose stated goal is to annihilate Zion.[20] Psalm 83 is either already fulfilled or in the process of being fulfilled. Therefore, we believe the next major event will be the War of Gog and Magog described in Ezekiel 38–39, which we believe will take place either before or at the beginning of the Tribulation. This would be the beginning of World War Three, followed by the Sixth-Trumpet War and ultimately, the Battle of Armageddon.

Many prophecy teachers have interpreted Ezekiel 38–39 as describing a Russian-led coalition of nations that attack Israel to "take booty" (Ezekiel 38:13 NKJV)—but God supernaturally intervenes, destroying the invading forces and protecting Israel.

"And it will come to pass at the same time, when Gog comes against the land of Israel," says the Lord GOD, "that My fury will show in My face. For in My jealousy and in the fire of My wrath I have spoken: 'Surely in that day there shall be a great earthquake in the land of Israel, so that the fish of the sea, the birds of the heavens, the beasts of the field, all creeping things that creep on the earth, and all men who are on the face of the earth shall shake at My presence. The mountains shall be thrown down, the steep places shall fall, and every wall shall fall to the ground.' I will call for a sword against Gog throughout all My mountains," says the Lord GOD. "Every man's sword will be against his brother. And I will bring him to judgment with pestilence and bloodshed; I will rain down on him, on his troops, and on the many peoples who are with him, flooding rain, great hailstones, fire, and brimstone. Thus I will magnify Myself and sanctify Myself, and I will be known in the eyes of many nations. Then they shall know that I am the LORD." (Ezekiel 38:18–23 NKJV)

Will Russia Nuke America?

When this war begins, Russia may destroy the United States through a nuclear attack. The late Chuck Missler once told me (Paul):

A third party is involved, a party that is not Gog and is not in Israel. A hailstone of fire will fall upon Gog and upon those who "dwell securely in the coastlands" [Ezekiel 39:6 ESV]. Who are they? We don't know. It's another party. One of the speculations is that it might be an occasion for an overdue judgment on the United States—that we start saber-rattling and we get hit as a bystander.

That gets to a whole other subject in terms of why the United States is ripe for judgment. Clearly, if you stand back and try to look at the United States as God would see it, we're dealing with a situation where we outlaw His Word in our schools, we will not allow His name to be used in public places, we do everything we can think of to insult Him. It's astonishing to see it as it would look from a God-fearing point of view. And so it's a very reasonable interrogation. Are we overdue for judgment? I would certainly think so.[21]

If the United States is destroyed in the War of Gog and Magog, this would leave a power vacuum on the planet. A time of crisis such as this could very well be what propels the Antichrist to prominence in global geopolitics, enabling him to sign a peace treaty with Israel, stopping the "overwhelming scourge" (Isaiah 28:18 NIV) and starting the Tribulation.

Many prophecy scholars believe the Rapture will happen simultaneously with the War of Gog and Magog and the destruction of America. We believe the War of Gog and Magog could be part of the fourth-seal judgment, in which a quarter of the world's population dies.

After that, construction of the third Jewish Temple (Daniel 9:27; Revelation 11:1) would begin, along with the formation of a global government (Daniel 2:40–44; 7:7, 23; Revelation 17:12), the rise of a universal religion (Revelation 17:1–5, 18; 13:11–17), the emergence of a global economic system (Revelation 13:15–18), Christ breaking the seven seals (Revelation 6; 8:1), and the seven trumpet judgments (Revelation 8–9).

The onslaught of these judgments would catapult the world into a state of chaos for the first half of the Tribulation. As you'll recall, the demonic creatures initially released from the "bottomless pit" are only allowed to torture people for five months, not kill them, and "only those men who do not have the seal of God on their foreheads" (Revelation 9:4 NIV).

So that raises some questions. Does this mean Christians have already gone to Heaven, or does it mean believers are still on Earth but they're not being attacked because they have the seal of God on their foreheads? If this is the case, is it possible that Christians aren't taken to Heaven until the midpoint of the Tribulation? Or perhaps some Christians are taken and others are left? We cannot say for certain.

As we've discussed, the second half of Revelation 9 involves the release of two hundred million demonic "horsemen" who kill a third of humanity. We believe the Sixth-Trumpet War allows the Antichrist and False Prophet to control the government and require everyone to take the mark of the beast (Revelation 13) or face decapitation (Revelation 20:4).

"For the Elect's Sake Those Days Will Be Shortened"

While we've long believed the Rapture takes place at the beginning of the Tribulation, a key question we should ask is whether believers could remain on Earth during the first half of the Tribulation. After all, Jesus said:

> "For then there will be great tribulation, such as has not been since the beginning of the world until this time, no, nor ever shall be. And unless those days were shortened, no flesh would be saved; but for the elect's sake those days will be shortened." (Matthew 24:21–22 NKJV)

When the Lord told me (Paul), "Revelation 9:11 [is] upon mankind," He didn't mean the Rapture is about to occur. He meant that all Hell is about to be unleashed. I (Paul) don't believe Christians will be here through the end of the Tribulation, but we should consider whether we could be here through the midpoint of it. Chuck Missler told me in 2015 that "Ezekiel 38–39" would be the next big event, "so keep your eye on Russia." He died in 2018; in early 2022, Russia attacked Ukraine.

Psalm 83 predicts that a coalition of nations will form to destroy Israel. As we were writing this chapter, the Palestinian terrorist group Hamas attacked Israel, killing more than a thousand civilians and 350 soldiers, shocking the world. About two hundred Israeli civilians and soldiers were taken as hostages to the Gaza Strip. Afterward, Israel struck back, and the situation was still escalating as this book went to press. Will this war expand into a larger regional war or even the War of Gog and Magog? Only time will tell, but Russia is currently building alliances with China, Iran, Syria, and other Middle Eastern nations.

A couple of months before that war broke out, eleven Russian and Chinese warships were spotted patrolling the coast of Alaska. In response, the United States Navy sent four destroyers to the area. U.S. Senator Dan Sullivan said the size of the joint operation was "unprecedented."[22]

Russian and Chinese warships in American waters? That's never happened before.[23]

CHAPTER TWELVE

The Third Temple, the Antichrist, and the Second Coming

*Let no one deceive you by any means; for that Day will
not come unless the falling away comes first, and the
man of sin is revealed, the son of perdition, who opposes
and exalts himself above all that is called God or that is
worshiped, so that he sits as God in the temple of God,
showing himself that he is God.*

—2 Thessalonians 2:3–4 NKJV

In a dream I (Paul) had on December 3, 2019, I saw the Antichrist—a man in his late thirties or early forties, with a thin build and dark hair—walk into the newly constructed Third Temple in Jerusalem in Israel.

As he strode into the main seating area, I saw many Jews dressed in ultra-orthodox attire waiting. It occurred to me that they didn't realize that man was the Antichrist. I then saw him walk behind the veil of the Holy of Holies and part the veil, exposing the Ark of the Covenant, Israel's most sacred object—built by Moses at God's direction to hold the tablets on which the Ten Commandments were inscribed, and the place from which God manifested His shekinah glory.

Astonishingly, I saw the man stand upon the Ark of the Covenant, in the middle of the mercy seat between the wings of the golden cherubim.

He turned to the people and said, "Where is your God?" He paused and then said, "I am your God."

At that point, the Jews in the temple realized that man was not their leader, but the Antichrist.

We believe this shocking act of desecrating the Third Temple—known as the "abomination that causes desolation" (Daniel 9:27 NIV)—will come midway through the Tribulation, shortly after Apollyon is released from the "bottomless pit" along with two hundred million demonic "horsemen" (Revelation 9:16 NKJV) who kill a third of humanity. By then, the whole world will be crying out for someone to stop the horrors—but the demons answer to the Antichrist. Dr. F. Kenton Beshore writes,

> When the Antichrist breaks the covenant with Israel in the middle of the Tribulation (Daniel 9:27) he launches a war of persecution against the Jews (Revelation 12:13). They flee from Satan and the Antichrist and through divine intervention they escape into the wilderness where they are protected for thirty-six months (Revelation 12:14).[1]

Revelation 11:7 says the "beast"—or Antichrist—"ascends out of the bottomless pit" (NKJV). This is part of Apollyon's mission: to unleash the "beast" from the gates of hell, allowing the devil to gain control of the world. At that point, Satan and all the other fallen angels will begin manifesting in the earthly realm, openly interacting with humans. In *The Final Nephilim*, Bible researcher Ryan Pitterson writes,

> Recall that, in the antediluvian era, open interaction between the angelic realm and humanity was commonplace. . . . However, at the fifth trumpet, the veil between the heavenly and earthly realms will start to recede with an onslaught of fallen angels. . . . The sinning sons of God, once rulers of

the planet and viewed as gods in the days of Noah, return as grotesque, hybrid, locust-like creatures in the end times.[2]

Angels and Demons

It's important to understand what the Bible says about the unusual abilities and characteristics of both angels and demons.

People who have encountered them tell me (Paul) that angels look like they're thirteen to fifteen feet tall. The Bible says people often fall on their faces, pass out, or tremble when they see a righteous angel sent by God to help people, because it's an entity greater than any human. That's why angels throughout the Bible often said things like, "Fear not. I'm a servant of the Lord." (Demons, however, don't say that. They come to torment people.)

Like angels, Nephilim are described as up to twelve feet tall. At only nine feet, Goliath was a small giant compared to what the ten spies saw when Joshua sent them to spy out the land of Canaan; the spies said, "We were like grasshoppers in our own sight, and so we were in their sight" (Numbers 13:33 NKJV).

Both good and fallen angels can take on different forms. The men of Sodom who saw the angels sent to rescue Lot and his family from the city thought they were normal men. Demons can also appear as extraterrestrials—little gray or green beings with big eyes who communicate telepathically. We believe people really are being abducted, really are being tormented, and think these entities are aliens—but they're really demons.

They can also appear like animals. The Apostle John wrote:

And I saw three unclean spirits like frogs coming out of the mouth of the dragon, out of the mouth of the beast, and out of the mouth of the false prophet. (Revelation 16:13 NKJV)

The Third Temple and the Antichrist

At the beginning of Revelation 11, an angel gives the Apostle John a reed and tells him to measure the temple, noting that the Gentiles will "trample on the holy city for forty-two months" (Revelation 11:2 NIV). Here we learn that the Third Temple will be built during the first half of the Tribulation, and at the midpoint, the Antichrist will enter it to commit the "abomination that causes desolation" (Daniel 9:27 NIV).

According to a poll of pastors conducted by Lifeway Research in 2016, 49 percent believe the Antichrist will arrive on the world scene at some point in the future, and 6 percent think he's already here.[3]

Meanwhile, many Jewish people are growing increasingly interested in rebuilding the Temple and resuming animal sacrifice there. The Temple Institute in Jerusalem has already made replicas of the sacred vessels used in the ancient Temple: the seven-branched candelabra, or Menorah; the golden Incense Altar; the golden Table of the Showbread; the sacred uniform of the *Kohen Gadol*, the High Priest; as well as the High Priest's *choshen* (breastplate), *ephod*, and *tzitz*; along with musical instruments the Levitical choir played.[4] As more Jews from around the world have returned to Israel in recent years, activists have begun reenacting the Passover sacrifice ceremony.[5]

But the Temple Mount in Jerusalem's Old City—the magnificent edifice where God, according to Jewish tradition, gathered the dust to create Adam, where Abraham nearly sacrificed Isaac to prove his faith, and where King Solomon built the First Temple—is the most hotly contested real estate on the planet. Not only is it the focus of Jewish history and biblical prophecies, but the location of two edifices that are sacred to Islam: Al-Aqsa Mosque and the Dome of the Rock.[6]

Retired U.S. Army Brigadier General Norman H. Andersson, author of *Jerusalem's Temple Now!*, says high-ranking political and military officials in Israel have told him that the movement to build the Third Temple is gaining significant momentum, with an estimated price tag of $2 billion. Anderson says these leaders told him that "when our religious leaders tell us that we should build the Temple, then we here at the Knesset will look at it to find out what we as politicians need to do."[7] There is enough room on the thirty-seven-acre Temple Mount to build the Third Temple and keep the Dome of the Rock and Al-Aqsa Mosque intact.

The Bible indicates that the Antichrist is the one who will success-fully negotiate an agreement bringing peace to the Middle East, which also permits the construction of the Third Temple.

"An Immortal Dictator"

The Bible contains many predictions that the Temple will be rebuilt in the end times. When the disciples asked about the signs of the "end of the age," Jesus told them to watch for an abomination that will take place in the "holy place."

> "So when you see standing in the holy place 'the abomina-tion that causes desolation,' spoken of through the prophet Daniel—let the reader understand—then let those who are in Judea flee to the mountains. . . . For then there will be great dis-tress, unequaled from the beginning of the world until now—and never to be equaled again." (Matthew 24:15–16, 21 NIV)

Ezekiel 37 speaks of the "dry bones" of Israel coming to life again in their own land. "Then the nations will know that I the LORD make Israel holy, when my sanctuary is among them forever" (Ezekiel 37:28 NIV).

However, the Apostle Paul warns that the Antichrist "will oppose and will exalt himself over everything that is called God or is wor-shiped, so that he sets himself up in God's temple, proclaiming himself to be God" (2 Thessalonians 2:4 NIV).

These and other verses reveal the Antichrist will have great diplomatic skill and broker a peace treaty between the Jews and Muslims that allows the Temple to be rebuilt. But then he himself will break the peace agreement by committing the "abomination that causes desolation" (Matthew 24:15 NIV) in which the "image of the beast" (Revelation 13:11–15 NKJV) is set up as an object of enforced global worship.

The curious remark about the "image of the beast" has raised questions in recent times about whether the Antichrist could be a transhuman being empowered by artificial intelligence: Elon Musk has said AI could create "an immortal dictator from which we could never escape."[8]

Restoring the Past

While visiting Jerusalem in the spring of 2015, I (Paul) met with Shalom Jerusalem Foundation President Rabbi Yehudah Glick. We discussed many things about Israel and Jerusalem, from both a political and biblical standpoint, including rebuilding the Third Temple on the Temple Mount. Since that time, Glick has become a member of the Knesset, run for president, and is now a leading activist for rebuilding the Third Temple.

I asked him where the temple would be built and what its dimensions would be. To my astonishment, he said Prime Minister Benjamin Netanyahu had already shown him the blueprints: It's a smaller version of Herod's Temple with no outer court. Interestingly, Revelation 11:2 says, "But leave out the court which is outside the temple, and do not measure it, for it has been given to the Gentiles. And they will tread the holy city underfoot for forty-two months" (NKJV). This confirmed to me how close we are to this major biblical milestone.

Also during that trip, I visited a Jewish farmer named Guy Urlich on the outskirts of Jericho, who was restoring balsam and frankincense trees, along with myrrh and spices. Since then, Urlich has been commissioned by the Sanhedrin to develop sacred incense to use in the Third Temple. We discussed several important archeological discoveries—including 1,500 pounds of incense from the Second Temple and the famous Copper Scroll, which was discovered along with the Dead Sea Scrolls in a cave near Qumran in 1952.

The Copper Scroll is a manuscript inscribed on thin sheets of nearly pure copper which details the purification ritual for priests who had become unclean through contact with dead animals during Temple sacrifices. This ritual involves the ashes of a red heifer—an unblemished animal that had never been hooked to a yoke—that was slaughtered and burned.[9]

From the time of Moses to the Second Temple period, red heifers were sacrificed nine times; according to Jewish prophecy, a tenth red heifer must be slaughtered and its ashes used to dedicate the site of the Third Temple—and that would only happen when the Messiah was about to appear.[10]

In 2022, a Texas rancher sent five perfect red heifers to Israel, heralding an event the nation had not seen for two thousand years.[11]

The Two Witnesses

After the Third Temple is built, Revelation 11:3 tells us God will send Two Witnesses to prophesy of the coming Messiah for three and a half years while clothed in sackcloth. They will have the power to shut the heavens and stop the rain. They will have the power to turn water into blood and smite the earth with plagues and other judgments. They will do that while proclaiming the Messiah's return. Government leaders will hate them for their powerful prophecies.

> When they finish their testimony, the beast that ascends out of the bottomless pit will make war against them, overcome them, and kill them. (Revelation 11:7 NKJV)

The bodies of the Two Witnesses will lie on the streets of Jerusalem for three and a half days, but people will refuse to bury them. People worldwide will celebrate their deaths by sending gifts to one another "because these two prophets had tormented those who live on the earth" (Revelation 11:10 NIV). Scripture says people all over the world will see their bodies. This is possible today thanks to television, the internet, smartphones, and satellites—further proof of the inerrant truth of the Bible.

> But after the three and a half days the breath of life from God entered them, and they stood on their feet, and terror struck those who saw them. (Revelation 11:11 NIV)

The entire world will witness the resurrection power of Jesus Christ as He raises the Two Witnesses from the dead. At that point, the Two Witnesses will hear a great voice from Heaven saying:

> "Come up here." And they ascended to heaven in a cloud, and their enemies saw them. In the same hour there was a great earthquake, and a tenth of the city fell. In the earthquake seven thousand people were killed, and the rest were afraid and gave glory to the God of heaven. (Revelation 11:12–13 NKJV)

It's possible that the Rapture won't happen until the Lord resurrects the Two Witnesses. It would make sense for all the Christians to be supernaturally transported to Heaven at the same time.

"Worthy to Escape All These Things"

In Luke 21:35–36, Jesus told His followers to watch for signs of His return, saying, "For it will come as a snare on all those who dwell on the face of the whole earth. Watch therefore, and pray always that you may be counted worthy to escape all these things that will come to pass, and to stand before the Son of Man" (NKJV).

Does this verse suggest a mid-Tribulation Rapture? Could it suggest that some people who believe they are going to Heaven in the Pretribulation Rapture could be left behind?

Today, many people profess faith in Christ but they're not totally sold-out, on-fire followers of Jesus. As we discussed previously, while nearly seven in ten American adults call themselves Christians, only a fraction have a biblical worldview; many hold syncretistic beliefs—a sort of "custom blend" of what they like from Christianity along with elements of Eastern mysticism, Marxism, moralistic therapeutic deism, nihilism, postmodernism, and secular humanism.[12]

"With such a worldview," writes Answers in Genesis founder Ken Ham, "there's no ultimate authority—'truth' is determined by whatever seems right to each person."[13]

Jesus told us to pray that we'd be "counted worthy to escape all these things" (Luke 21:36 NKJV). You don't want to be here during the Tribulation, but the truth is, only God knows when the Rapture will take place, so the wisest thing is to make sure you're right with God. Ask Jesus to forgive you of your sins and seek His destiny for your life, one decision at a time, relying on His written and spoken Word to do so. (Those two things will never contradict each other. Test everything you hear in the Spirit, in your mind, or from another person by the Word of God.)

We live in a time of mass deception. Today, only 2 percent of Americans believe they will go to Hell when they die, while 48 percent believe that if a person is generally good, or does good things, they can "earn" a place in Heaven.[14] That's a lie from the devil. Not all paths lead to Heaven. Jesus said, "*I* am the way and the truth and the life. No one comes to the Father except through me" (John 14:6 NIV; emphasis added).

When the Rapture occurs, we believe a lot of people—perhaps many who say they are Christians—are going to be left behind, saying, "I thought I was going to go with the rest of them."

This, says Arizona Christian University president Len Munsil, should serve as "a wakeup call for the church, and for leaders in all areas of influence, to speak, teach, and work to restore biblical truth."[15]

In addition, many more people will likely be fooled by the way we believe the Antichrist might explain the Rapture to those left behind, perhaps saying, "We told you the aliens were coming. They took the Christians away because they weren't ready to evolve to a higher level of consciousness." Then he will require everyone to take the "mark of the beast" to avoid a similar fate.

Sometimes people get confused about whether they may already have inadvertently taken "the mark," so it's important to understand what the Bible says about it.

"No one's going to take it by accident because you might say, 'Well, I was at Disneyland the other day and I wanted to leave the park and they stamped my hand. Have I received the mark of the beast?' No," says Laurie, "you've received the mark of the mouse." But unlike that washable hand stamp, "you will do it willingly. It'll be [taken] as a sign of devotion to Antichrist. It will be your passport to [conduct] commerce. It's very simple. If you take the mark, you can function. If you don't, you won't be able to."[16]

Laurie cautions against spending too much energy trying to figure out all the details of who the Antichrist is or what the mark will be. "The Bible doesn't tell you to be looking for Antichrist. It tells you to be looking for Jesus Christ," he says. "[The] restraining force in the world today is the work of the Holy Spirit through the Church. When the Church is removed, then Antichrist will be revealed."[17]

Seven Bowls of God's Wrath

As the "mark of the beast" system is implemented, the Great Tribulation—the last half of the seven-year Tribulation—begins. During this time, the seven bowls of God's wrath are poured out upon the world, breaking the government, economic, and religious system of the Antichrist and False Prophet.

> Then I saw another sign in heaven, great and marvelous: seven angels having the seven last plagues, for in them the wrath of God is complete. . . . After these things I looked, and behold, the temple of the tabernacle of the testimony in heaven was opened. And out of the temple came the seven angels having the seven plagues, clothed in pure bright linen, and having their chests girded with golden bands. Then one of the four living creatures gave to the seven angels seven golden bowls full of the wrath of God who lives forever and ever. (Revelation 15:1, 5–7 NKJV)

Revelation 16 describes the various judgments, including:

- First Bowl: A "foul and loathsome sore" breaks out on those who took the "mark of the beast" and those who worshiped his image. (Revelation 16:2 NKJV)
- Second Bowl: The oceans become like the "blood as of a dead man" and many sea creatures die. (Revelation 16:3 NKJV)
- Third Bowl: The rivers and springs become "blood." (Revelation 16:4 NKJV)
- Fourth Bowl: The sun scorches men with "great heat." They curse God, but refuse to repent. (Revelation 16:9 NKJV)

- Fifth Bowl: The beast's kingdom becomes "full of darkness; and they gnawed their tongues because of the pain." (Revelation 16:10 NKJV)
- Sixth Bowl: The Euphrates River dries up, allowing the "kings of the earth" to gather for the Battle of Armageddon. (Revelation 16:12–16 NKJV)
- Seventh Bowl: Cosmic signs, including "noises and thunderings and lightnings" break out, accompanied by the most powerful earthquake of all time. The seas rise and the mountains fall; the most massive hailstorm of all time occurs, with "great hail," each "about the weight of a talent" (i.e., one hundred pounds) falling on people. (Revelation 16:17–21 NIV)

Battle of Armageddon and the Second Coming

Now the stage is set for the Battle of Armageddon. The Bible tells us this will take place in the plain of Esdraelon, about fifty miles north of Jerusalem. This is where the armies of the world will wage war on the returning forces of Jesus Christ at the Second Coming.[18] Daniel 11:40–45, Joel 3:9–17, Zechariah 14:1–3, and Revelation 16:14–16 all tell us the kings of the world will gather their armies near the hill of Megiddo, the scene of many Old Testament battles, for this great battle. The Antichrist will defeat the armies from the south and will destroy a "revived Babylon in the east before finally turning his forces toward Jerusalem to subdue and destroy it."[19] At this point, Christ will return to rescue His people in Israel, and He and His angelic armies will destroy the enemy forces, capture the Antichrist and False Prophet, and ultimately cast them into the Lake of Fire (Revelation 19:11–21).[20]

Now I saw heaven opened, and behold, a white horse. And He who sat on him was called Faithful and True, and in righteousness He judges and makes war. His eyes were like a flame of fire, and on His head were many crowns. He had a name written that no one knew except Himself. He was clothed with a robe dipped in blood, and His name is called The Word of God. And the armies in heaven, clothed in fine linen, white and clean, followed Him on white horses. Now out of His mouth goes a sharp sword, that with it He should strike the nations. And He Himself will rule them with a rod of iron. He Himself treads the winepress of the fierceness and wrath of Almighty God. And He has on His robe and on His thigh a name written:

KING OF KINGS AND LORD OF LORDS. . . .

Then I saw the beast and the kings of the earth and their armies gathered together to make war against the rider on the horse and against His army. But the beast was captured, and with it the false prophet who had performed the signs on its behalf. With these signs he had deluded those who had received the mark of the beast and worshiped its image. The two of them were thrown alive into the fiery lake of burning sulfur. The rest were killed with the sword coming out of the mouth of the rider on the horse. (Revelation 19:11–16, 19–21 NIV)

CHAPTER THIRTEEN

God's Prophetic Timing: What's Next?

*It is the hope of the Second Coming of Christ that thrills
me every day of my life. I know that He's coming again,
and I know that He's going to set up a kingdom of
which there will be no end.*

—Billy Graham

We are living during the final moments of God's prophetic count-down, a time when the "shakings" are intensifying.

I (Paul) have been asking God what we can do. We can't stop biblical prophecies from unfolding, but we can repent of our sins, turn to Him, and pray for our brothers and sisters around the world who are suffering in various ways, whether they are victims of sex trafficking or casualties of war.

At Billy Graham's funeral in 2018, Jim Bakker asked Graham's son, Franklin, what he thought his father's death meant prophetically.

"It's about to be released," Bakker recalls Franklin telling him. "The demons of hell are about to be unleashed upon the earth."[1]

I agree with that: Thirty years ago, I had a dream in which I saw seven men praying in the basement of a church. One was Pope John Paul II; one was Billy Graham; one was Dr. Lester Sumrall; one was Oral Roberts; and the other three were people I didn't recognize who were dressed in the religious attire of the Greek Orthodox, Coptic Christian, and Orthodox Jewish faiths.

As I was watched, one by one, they began falling dead. First was Sumrall, then Roberts, then the pope, then the others I didn't recognize. Graham was the last one standing.

He continued to pray for a while. When he finally did fall, the Lord told me, "Run outside and start ringing the bell." So I ran outside, where I found an old church bell on a pole and started ringing it.

The Lord said, "Proclaim that the time is near. Proclaim that the time is near."

It's been several years now since Graham died, and what's happening around the world in a prophetic sense is incredible. The events foretold in the book of Revelation are about to come to pass.

Prophetic Words

As I mentioned earlier, in 2015, I had the privilege of interviewing Chuck Missler on my YouTube channel. When I asked him which end-time event would happen next, he said it would be Russia invading Ukraine.

Similarly, Jack Van Impe—end-times expert and host of the weekly television show *Jack Van Impe Presents*—called me in late 2019 after watching one of my YouTube videos. I'd never met him but had watched him on television since I was a boy. He was lying in bed, very ill, at the time. He said, "I like what you're doing, young man." (I felt good about the fact that he called me "young man.")

"Keep talking about current events," he said. "Keep telling people to be saved. They're about ready to build a Third Temple. There's going to be some things that happen first, but then they're going to build it.

"Paul, you're going to see it," he concluded. "I want to see it, too. I hope God lets me live, but I don't think He will."

Six weeks later, he died.

Around that time, I had lunch with Dr. Irvin Baxter Jr.—host of the internationally syndicated biblical prophecy television program *End of the Age*. It would turn out to be our final meeting.

We talked for three hours about the Bible and the Second Coming. Baxter had long believed he would be a part of a move of God in Jerusalem, but "If I don't make it, Paul," he said, "you will. I need you to help."

I said, "Lord willing, if I'm still above ground, I'll help."

Baxter invited me to go with him to his office in downtown Jerusalem, which has a view of the Dome of the Rock and the Temple Mount. He said, "I plan on sitting at my desk and watching them build the Third Temple."

A few months later, COVID lockdowns began to impact the world, preventing us from having that meeting in his office. On September 15, 2020, President Donald Trump oversaw the signing of the Abraham Accords between Israel, Bahrain, and the United Arab Emirates. I called Dr. Baxter a few days later and said, "You were right, they did sign the agreement in 2020. What's next? Is this the beginning of the Tribulation? Or are they going to build the Third Temple first? Or are we about to have the Rapture? Or are we getting ready for the 'great falling away'? Or should we prepare for the great end-time harvest?"

He said: "Paul, I will tell you exactly after the election."

Dr. Baxter died on November 3, 2020—the day of the presidential election, shortly before he was scheduled to come on my show to answer that question.

God's timing is His timing, not our timing. We just have to be ready.

New Heaven, New Earth, and New Jerusalem

In the meantime, we can take comfort in knowing that after the Battle of Armageddon, Jesus Christ will rule on Earth as the King of Kings and Lord of Lords for a thousand years—a time of unprecedented peace and true justice.

And I saw an angel coming down out of heaven, having the
key to the Abyss and holding in his hand a great chain. He
seized the dragon, that ancient serpent, who is the devil, or
Satan, and bound him for a thousand years. He threw him
into the Abyss, and locked and sealed it over him, to keep
him from deceiving the nations anymore until the thousand
years were ended. After that, he must be set free for a short
time.

I saw thrones on which were seated those who had been
given authority to judge. And I saw the souls of those who
had been beheaded because of their testimony about Jesus
and because of the word of God. They had not worshiped
the beast or its image and had not received its mark on their
foreheads or their hands. They came to life and reigned with
Christ a thousand years. (The rest of the dead did not come
to life until the thousand years were ended.) This is the first
resurrection. Blessed and holy are those who share in the first
resurrection. The second death has no power over them, but
they will be priests of God and of Christ and will reign with
him for a thousand years. (Revelation 20:1–6 NIV)

When that time is over, Satan will be released from the Abyss
and given an opportunity to deceive the nations and gather them for
battle once again. This will be followed by the Great White Throne
Judgment.

They marched across the breadth of the earth and surrounded
the camp of God's people, the city he loves. But fire came
down from heaven and devoured them. And the devil, who
deceived them, was thrown into the lake of burning sulfur,

where the beast and the false prophet had been thrown. They will be tormented day and night for ever and ever.

Then I saw a great white throne and him who was seated on it. The earth and the heavens fled from his presence, and there was no place for them. And I saw the dead, great and small, standing before the throne, and books were opened. Another book was opened, which is the book of life. The dead were judged according to what they had done as recorded in the books. The sea gave up the dead that were in it, and death and Hades gave up the dead that were in them, and each person was judged according to what they had done. Then death and Hades were thrown into the lake of fire. The lake of fire is the second death. Anyone whose name was not found written in the book of life was thrown into the lake of fire. (Revelation 20:9–15 NIV)

Revelation 21 describes the eternal home of those who have accepted Jesus as their Savior.

Then I saw "a new heaven and a new earth," for the first heaven and the first earth had passed away, and there was no longer any sea. I saw the Holy City, the new Jerusalem, coming down out of heaven from God, prepared as a bride beautifully dressed for her husband. And I heard a loud voice from the throne saying, "Look! God's dwelling place is now among the people, and he will dwell with them. They will be his people, and God himself will be with them and be their God. 'He will wipe every tear from their eyes. There will be no more death' or mourning or crying or pain, for the old order of things has passed away."

He who was seated on the throne said, "I am making everything new!" Then he said, "Write this down, for these words are trustworthy and true."

He said to me: "It is done. I am the Alpha and the Omega, the Beginning and the End. To the thirsty I will give water without cost from the spring of the water of life. Those who are victorious will inherit all this, and I will be their God and they will be my children. But the cowardly, the unbelieving, the vile, the murderers, the sexually immoral, those who practice magic arts, the idolaters and all liars—they will be consigned to the fiery lake of burning sulfur. This is the second death."

One of the seven angels who had the seven bowls full of the seven last plagues came and said to me, "Come, I will show you the bride, the wife of the Lamb." And he carried me away in the Spirit to a mountain great and high, and showed me the Holy City, Jerusalem, coming down out of heaven from God. (Revelation 21:1–10 NIV)

The last chapter of the Bible, Revelation 22, describes how the Garden of Eden is restored in Heaven. There, believers will worship the Lord and help administrate the universe in a place where "eye has not seen, nor ear heard, nor have entered into the heart of man the things which God has prepared for those who love Him" (1 Corinthians 2:9 NKJV).

The Bible concludes with this encouraging message from Jesus:

"Look, I am coming soon! My reward is with me, and I will give to each person according to what they have done. I am the Alpha and the Omega, the First and the Last, the Beginning and the End.

"Blessed are those who wash their robes, that they may have the right to the tree of life and may go through the gates into the city. Outside are the dogs, those who practice magic arts, the sexually immoral, the murderers, the idolaters and everyone who loves and practices falsehood.

"I, Jesus, have sent my angel to give you this testimony for the churches. I am the Root and the Offspring of David, and the bright Morning Star."

The Spirit and the bride say, "Come!" And let the one who hears say, "Come!" Let the one who is thirsty come; and let the one who wishes take the free gift of the water of life. . . .

He who testifies to these things says, "Yes, I am coming soon." (Revelation 22:12–17, 20 NIV)

The "Great Harvest Revival" and You

*"Behold, I say to you, lift up your eyes and look at the
fields, for they are already white for harvest!"*

—John 4:35 NKJV

*"For this year," sayeth the Lord, "is the beginning of the
final harvest. This is not revival; it is a movement to bring
in the souls of men from every country. For America is
not the only country that I am reaching for. I will renew
my covenant with her first," says the Lord, "but it will be
the beginning of the release of the glory of God."*

—Kent Christmas

What do you do now? What assignments has He created you to
carry out?

You've read *Revelation 911*, you now understand what's really happening and what's ahead, and perhaps the Holy Spirit is stirring your
heart. So what does the Heavenly Commander-in-Chief want you to
do in the time left before His return?

This is the moment when the army of God arises, exerts its
authority over spiritual darkness, and helps bring in the great harvest.
It's a time of miracles, signs, and wonders. This is it. This is our time.

The prophet Joel, God's spokesman during the reign of King Joash from 835–796 BC, spoke about the "latter rain"—the end-times revival.

> "And afterward, I will pour out my Spirit on all people. Your sons and daughters will prophesy, your old men will dream dreams, your young men will see visions. Even on my servants, both men and women, I will pour out my Spirit in those days. I will show wonders in the heavens and on the earth, blood and fire and billows of smoke. The sun will be turned to darkness and the moon to blood before the coming of the great and dreadful day of the LORD. And everyone who calls on the name of the LORD will be saved." (Joel 2:28–32 NIV)

As this movement unfolds, we must ask: What is the Church's role? What do we as the Church, as believers, do? Do we just throw up our hands in defeat, or do we pray, fast, put on the full armor of God (Ephesians 6:10–18), and stand up for what we believe? Do we hold huge rallies? Do we have large prayer vigils?

The answer is: We get serious—and we get busy. We pray, fast, and cry out to God for His will to be done in our nation while we share the Gospel with everyone we can reach. We hold large gatherings—and small ones. Everyone puts their hand to the plow in whatever measure of influence they have been given. We start having major victories and then the "former" and "latter rain" start to fall.

In Joel 2:25 God says: "I will repay you for the years the locusts have eaten" (NIV). We believe it means we're going to have a time of repentance and awakening around the world.

The Return: National and Global Day of Prayer and Repentance

September 26, 2020, marked the first day of national repentance decreed by the federal government since the Lincoln administration. About 250,000 people gathered on the National Mall in Washington, D.C., for an event called The Return: National and Global Day of Prayer and Repentance. About forty-two million people watched it via simulcast, making it the largest livestreaming viewership in Christian history.[1]

This was followed by another event held on January 8, 2022, in Florida called The Renewal: Restoring America's Founding Covenant. On this day, faith leaders renewed the covenant the Pilgrims made with God four centuries ago, which dedicated America to the "glory of God, and advancement of the Christian faith."[2]

It was the second step in the five-step biblical renewal process (Repentance, Reconciliation, Restoration, Revival, Reformation) that the ancient Israelites followed during times of national crisis.[3] As this book went to press, more events were being planned, including "The Return Israel" in Jerusalem.

"The Renewal is about restoring our covenant with God," says The Return Israel cofounder Kevin Jessip. "It started with The Return with repentance, and now we're going through reconciliation and restoration, which is renewing the covenant we broke with Almighty God. In The Renewal, we are saying, 'Lord, have mercy on us in the midst of the redemptive judgments happening.' The fires, plagues, floods, and everything we are seeing are no different than the redemptive judgments ancient Egypt experienced. The Renewal is a reconciliation and restoration of the covenant, which is part of returning to God. I believe after this the revival is coming."[4]

We agree. The revival won't last forever—maybe only a few years—but it will come if we truly repent and humble ourselves before the Lord.

> Repent ye therefore, and be converted, that your sins may be blotted out, when the times of refreshing shall come from the presence of the Lord.
>
> And he shall send Jesus Christ, which before was preached unto you:
>
> Whom the heaven must receive until the times of restitution of all things, which God hath spoken by the mouth of all his holy prophets since the world began. (Acts 3:19–21 KJV)

This doesn't mean the forces of darkness will relent from their crusade of evil, or that globalists are going to cancel the Great Reset or stop doing everything they can to prepare the world for the arrival of the Antichrist and False Prophet.

Rather, as the Lord pours out His Spirit upon the world, and revival and awakening sweep the globe as part of the "final harvest," we'll see an acceleration of end-times events taking place simultaneously. The final harvest is going to be massive because the Lord says it's not His will that any should perish but that all should come to repentance (2 Peter 3:9). Therefore, His extension of grace will be colossal.

This is why I (Paul) believe the Church may be here until the Two Witnesses are taken to Heaven. Only the Church has the power to deliver. Only the Church has the Holy Spirit. Only the Church brings the message of salvation.

The Apostle John said there will be no way to count how many people become believers during the Tribulation. We believe more people are going to get saved during the first three and a half years of the Tribulation than in the rest of history combined.

The Great Harvest won't be started by one ministry or preacher, but through a spirit of revival that will spread around the globe, inspired by the Holy Spirit.

We're already hearing reports of it. For example, Greg Laurie baptized 4,500 people over a weekend in 2023 in Newport Beach, California, the birthplace of the Jesus Movement. The "Jesus Revolution Baptism" followed the SoCal Harvest Crusade in Anaheim, at which 6,794 of the 32,500 attendees decided to dedicate their lives to Jesus.[5]

This followed reports of large-scale baptisms across the country, along with the Asbury Revival, involving mostly Asbury University students that went on for weeks in Kentucky in early 2023.[6] Tens of thousands of other people gathered at outdoor events led by worship artist Sean Feucht across the nation, and there have been reports of other revivals taking place around the world.[7]

Satan hates this. That's why he's going to launch the greatest assault in history against the Church. His counterattack will involve releasing Apollyon from the "bottomless pit" along with the demons of Hell.

But our God is stronger than we can imagine. Tribulation saints will have the seal of God on their foreheads. Jesus said,

> "Do not be afraid of what you are about to suffer. I tell you, the devil will put some of you in prison to test you, and you will suffer persecution for ten days. Be faithful, even to the point of death, and I will give you life as your victor's crown." (Revelation 2:10 NIV)

He also said, "But the one who stands firm to the end will be saved" (Matthew 24:13 NIV).

Hold fast. Don't plan what you'll say when people confront you. Let the Holy Spirit speak through you at the time (Mark 13:11).

Believers should follow the model of the early Church. They experienced some of the greatest persecution in history: The Romans fed them to the lions. They made them face armed gladiators and fight to the death. They crucified them. They dismembered them. They did all kinds of terrible things to them, but the whole time the Christians were growing in numbers, evangelizing, and moving all over the world, taking the Gospel with them. The devil couldn't stop them.

Although there will be great adversities to overcome in the days ahead, there will also be tremendous victories and miracles—including massive numbers of salvation experiences—until the Lord returns.

Jesus offers an encouraging word about that: In the end, truth, love, and good prevail over evil.

> "Look, I am coming soon! My reward is with me, and I will give to each person according to what they have done. I am the Alpha and the Omega, the First and the Last, the Beginning and the End.
>
> "Blessed are those who wash their robes, that they may have the right to the tree of life and may go through the gates into the city." (Revelation 22:12–14 NIV)

Prayer of Salvation

This prayer of salvation is a personal and heartfelt one that is often used in Christian traditions as a way for individuals to express their belief in Jesus Christ and invite Him into their lives.

While there are different variations of this prayer, the essence remains the same—it's a sincere declaration of one's faith in and desire for a personal relationship with Jesus. Feel free to express these thoughts in your own words as you talk with Him.

> *Dear Lord Jesus, I come to You today as a sinner in need of Your forgiveness. I believe that You are the Son of God, that You died on the cross for my sins, and that You rose again from the dead. I acknowledge that I have fallen short of Your perfection, and I repent of my sins.*
>
> *I invite You into my heart and life, to be my Lord and Savior. I turn away from my old ways and choose to follow You.*

Please cleanse me, forgive me, and make me new. Fill me with Your Holy Spirit and guide me in the path of righteousness. Thank You for Your grace, Your love, and Your salvation. I trust in You alone for my eternal life. Help me to live for You and to walk in Your ways. In Jesus's name, I pray. Amen.

Remember, the words themselves are not as important as the sincerity and conviction behind them. This prayer is a personal expression of faith and a way to open your heart to the transforming power of God's love. If you have questions, consider reaching out to a pastor or spiritual leader in your community, or contact us (either www.paulbegleyprophecy.com or www.troyanderson.us will work). We'd be happy to share your joy in becoming a follower of Jesus and to pray for you.

About the Authors

Paul Begley's gifting lies in evangelism and Bible prophecy. By the grace of God, tens of thousands have come to Jesus Christ through his ministry as a pastor and host of the syndicated television show and YouTube channel The Coming Apocalypse. He is a fourth-generation preacher whose great-grandfather was part of the Azusa Street Revival. Begley was ordained by Dr. Lester Sumrall, founder of the Lester Sumrall Evangelistic Association in South Bend, Indiana. He studied at Indiana Christian University and under Pastor Charles Begley at Community Gospel Baptist Church in Knox, Indiana. Begley first caught the world's attention in 2011 with prophecies that were featured in *TIME*, *Newsweek*, on CNN, and in other mainstream media outlets.

The Coming Apocalypse television program reaches fifty million homes, and Begley's YouTube channel has more than 365,000 subscribers. In addition, Begley hosts an internet radio talk show several times a week that can be heard around the world.

Begley and his wife, Heidi, have been married for nearly forty years. They have three sons and seven grandchildren. Learn more at www. paulbegleyprophecy.org.

Troy Anderson is a Pulitzer Prize–nominated investigative journalist, bestselling author, founder of the Inspire Literary Group, vice president of Battle Ready Ministries, executive editor of The Return International, former executive editor of *Charisma* magazine and Charisma Media, speaker, and television and radio commentator.

He spent two decades working as a reporter, bureau chief, and editorial writer at the *Los Angeles Daily News*, the *Press-Enterprise*, and other newspapers. He currently writes for Reuters, Newsmax, Townhall, *Christianity Today*, *Charisma*, Charisma News, *Human Events, American Spectator, Outreach*, and other media outlets. He's the founder and editor-in-chief of Prophecy Investigators, an online news magazine.

He appears regularly on Newsmax TV, CBN News, BlazeTV, GOD TV, Real America's Voice, Daystar Television Network's *Joni Table Talk* and *Ministry Now, Tipping Point with Jimmy Evans, Jewish Voice with Jonathan Bernis, The Jim Bakker Show*, SkyWatch TV, Cornerstone TV Network's *Real-Life* show, and many nationally syndicated radio programs and YouTube shows. He lives with his family in Irvine, California. Find out more at www.troyanderson.us and www. inspireliterary.com.

Notes

Introduction: "The Hour Is Coming. It Is Upon Mankind."

1. Hugh Ross, "Fulfilled Prophecy: Evidence for the Reliability of the Bible," Reasons to Believe, August 22, 2023, https://reasons.org/explore/publications/articles/fulfilled-prophecy-evidence-for-the-reliability-of-the-bible.
2. William F. Jasper, "Biden's ESG Agenda," *The New American* 39, no. 8 (April 24, 2023), https://thenewamerican.com/print/bidens-esg-agenda.
3. Thomas Ice, "God's Purpose for Israel During the Tribulation," Liberty University Pre-Trib Research Center, May 1, 2009, https://digitalcommons.liberty.edu/cgi/viewcontent.cgi?article=1121&context=pretrib_arch.

Chapter One: Ground Zero of the Apocalypse

1. James F. Fitzgerald, *The 9/11 Prophecy: Startling Evidence the End Times Have Begun* (Washington, D.C.: WND Books, 2013), v–vi.
2. GODSPEED Magazine, "Will the World Turn Back to God?," YouTube, 20:24, September 4, 2020, https://www.youtube.com/watch?v=4M5nN2ezZSc&t=10s.
3. Henry H. Halley, *Halley's Bible Handbook*, 25th ed. (Grand Rapids: Zondervan, 2007), 878.

4. Charlotte Morabito, "Nearly 70% of Americans Are Worried about a Nuclear Attack, According to APA Survey. Here's What Could Happen," CNBC, April 5, 2022, https://www.cnbc.com/2022/04/05/hypothetical-nuclear-attack.html.

5. Aaron Earls, "Vast Majority of Pastors See Signs of End Times in Current Events," Lifeway Research, April 7, 2020, https://research.lifeway.com/2020/04/07/vast-majority-of-pastors-see-signs-of-end-times-in-current-events.

6. Joel C. Rosenberg, "EXCLUSIVE POLL: What Do Americans Think about Iran, Russia, COVID and Bible Prophecy?," The Joshua Fund, April 2022, https://www.joshuafund.com/learn/latest-news/exclusive-national-poll.

7. "WHO Coronavirus (COVID-19) Dashboard," World Health Organization, https://covid19.who.int/?mapFilter=deaths.

8. Andrew Roth, "Putin Compares Himself to Peter the Great in Quest to Take Back Russian Lands," *The Guardian*, June 10, 2022, https://www.theguardian.com/world/2022/jun/10/putin-compares-himself-to-peter-the-great-in-quest-to-take-back-russian-lands.

9. Simina Mistreanu, "China Releases TV Documentary Showcasing Army's Ability to Attack Taiwan," Associated Press, August 6, 2023, https://apnews.com/article/china-taiwan-documentary-attack-invasion-chasing-dreams-4105d5f0bde59337d90f1e67d149b32c.

10. Jon Gambrell, "Iran Has Enough Enriched Uranium to Build 'Several' Nuclear Weapons, UN Says," *PBS NewsHour*, January 26, 2023, https://www.pbs.org/newshour/world/iran-could-build-several-nuclear-weapons-un-says.

11. Bruce W. Bennett, "How Kim Jong-un's Fears Shape North Korea's Nuclear Weapons Agenda," The RAND Blog, April 19, 2023, https://www.rand.org/blog/2023/04/how-kim-jong-uns-fears-shape-north-koreas-nuclear-weapons.html.

12. Battle Ready Ministries, "Are We on the Verge of World War III? Lt. General Jerry Boykin|FrontLine Battle Ready Ministries (#51)," YouTube, 27:38, March 20, 2023, https://www.youtube.com/watch?v=59bPwKvnszk.

13. Edith M. Lederer, "UN Chief Warns World Is One Step from 'Nuclear Annihilation,'" Associated Press, August 1, 2022, https://apnews.com/article/russia-ukraine-covid-health-antonio-guterres-2871563e530f9a676d7884b3e2d871c3.

14. Anisha Kohli, "The Doomsday Clock Is Closer to Catastrophe than Ever Before," *TIME*, January 24, 2023, https://time.com/6249856/doomsday-clock-catastrophe-ukraine.

15. Greg Bruno, "Even a Nuclear Conflict between New Nuclear States Would Decimate Crop Production and Result in Widespread Starvation," Rutgers University, August 15, 2022, https://www.rutgers.edu/news/nuclear-war -would-cause-global-famine-and-kill-billions-rutgers-led-study-finds.

16. Miriam Fauzia, "Fact Check: Quarantine 'Camps' Are Real, but COVID-19 Camp Claim Stretches Truth," *USA Today*, updated August 11, 2020, https:// www.usatoday.com/story/news/factcheck/2020/08/09/fact-check-quarantine -sites-real-covid-19-claim-stretches-truth/5499196002.

17. Troy Anderson, "The Armageddon Vaccine," *Godspeed Magazine*, June 2020.

18. "Our Mission," About Us, World Economic Forum, accessed November 5, 2023, https://www.weforum.org/about/world-economic-forum.

19. Terry Chan and Alexandra Dimitrijevic, "Global Debt Leverage: Is a Great Reset Coming?," S&P Global, January 13, 2023, https://www.spglobal.com /en/research-insights/featured/special-editorial/look-forward/global-debt -leverage-is-a-great-reset-coming.

20. Jeffrey A. Tucker, "Why You're Feeling So Much Poorer," *Epoch Times*, updated September 10, 2023, https://www.theepochtimes.com/opinion/why -you-are-feeling-so-much-poorer-5483280.

21. Ronaldo Marquez, "US Banking Crisis Worsens with Half of America's Banks on the Verge of Failure," NewsBTC, May 2, 2023, https://www .newsbtc.com/breaking-news-ticker/us-banking-crisis-worsens-with-half-of -americas-banks-on-the-verge-of-failure.

22. Kelvin Chan and Paul Wiseman, "Wheat and Barley Shortage: How Russia-Ukraine War Triggered a Global Food Crisis," Fox 11 Los Angeles, June 18, 2022, https://www.foxla.com/news/wheat-barley-shortage-russia-ukraine -war-trigger-food-crisis.

23. Mark Hitchcock, *The End* (Carol Stream, Illinois: Tyndale Momentum, 2018), 283.

24. Bill Gates, "Bill Gates: 'I Worry We're Making the Same Mistakes Again,'" *New York Times*, March 19, 2023, https://www.nytimes.com/2023/03/19/ opinion/bill-gates-pandemic-preparedness-covid.html.

25. Marc Lallanilla, "The Next Pandemic 'Even Deadlier' than COVID Is Coming, Warns WHO," *New York Post*, updated May 24, 2023, https:// nypost.com/2023/05/23/pandemic-even-deadlier-than-covid-is-coming -warns-who.

26. Rhonda Empson, "Dream for Paul Begley . . . ," YouTube, 5:42, March 15, 2021, https://www.youtube.com/watch?v=rEDTwqVljKo. Empson's

collection of videos recording her dreams throughout 2018 was later wiped out. After having a similar dream in 2021, she posted a second video in which she related the details of both.

27. Vijdan Mohammad Kawoosa, "10,000 Tremors: How Turkey Has Been Rattled by Aftershocks since the Feb. 6 Earthquake," Reuters, March 1, 2023, https://www.reuters.com/graphics/TURKEY-QUAKE/AFTERSHOCKS/dwpkdzklevm.

28. Emanuel Fabian and Alexander Fulbright, "Palestinians Say 11 Killed, 102 Hurt in Nablus Clashes Between Gunmen, Israeli Forces," *The Times of Israel*, February 22, 2023, https://www.timesofisrael.com/5-palestinians-said-killed-in-nablus-amid-clashes-between-gunmen-israeli-forces.

29. News Wires, "'They Burned Everything': Israeli Settlers Torch Palestinian Homes, Cars after West Bank Attack," France 24, February 27, 2023, https://www.france24.com/en/middle-east/20230227-palestinians-count-cost-of-israeli-settler-reprisals-with-deadly-west-bank-attack.

Chapter Two: Understanding Future Events from Fulfilled Prophecies

1. Saddleback Church, "The Case for Christmas | Worship Service | Lee Strobel," YouTube, 1:10:24, December 5, 2021, https://www.youtube.com/watch?v=WbEaoCwYrMQ.

2. Peter Stoner, *Science Speaks: Scientific Proof of the Accuracy of Prophecy and the Bible* (Chicago: Moody Publishers), quoted in Jesus Film Project, "55 Old Testament Prophecies about Jesus," *Evangelism Blog,* November 17, 2021, https://www.jesusfilm.org/blog/old-testament-prophecies.

3. Saddleback Church, "'The Case for Christmas' with Lee Strobel," YouTube, December 7, 2021, https://www.youtube.com/watch?v=stoqm4ffjUI.

4. Dave Hunt, *A Woman Rides the Beast* (Eugene, Oregon: Harvest House Publishers, 1994), 20.

5. Ibid.

6. Hugh Ross, interview by Troy Anderson, April 26, 2023.

7. Mark Hitchcock, *The End* (Carol Stream, Illinois: Tyndale Momentum, 2018), 4.

8. Ross, interview.

9. *Britannica Online*, s.v. "Babylonian Captivity," accessed November 5, 2023, https://www.britannica.com/event/Babylonian-Captivity.

10. Ibid.

11. Tim LaHaye and Thomas Ice, *Charting the End Times* (Eugene, Oregon: Harvest House Publishers, 2001), 14.

12. Andrew MacDonald and Ed Stetzer, "The Lasting Legacy of the Jesus People: How an Unlikely, Countercultural Movement Went Mainstream," *Talbot Magazine*, Biola University, June 17, 2020, https://www.biola.edu/blogs/talbot-magazine/2020/the-lasting-legacy-of-the-jesus-people.

13. U.S. Geological Survey, "How Many Active Volcanoes Are There on Earth?," July 6, 2017, https://www.usgs.gov/faqs/how-many-active-volcanoes-are-there-earth#:~:text=There%20are%20about%201%2C350%20potentially,have%20erupted%20in%20historical%20time.

14. "Hunga Tonga-Hunga Ha'apai Eruption," NASA Jet Propulsion Laboratory, August 8, 2023, https://www.jpl.nasa.gov/images/pia26006-hunga-tonga-hunga-haapai-eruption.

15. Jennifer Nalewicki, "'Mind Boggling Array' of 19,000 Undersea Volcanoes Discovered with High-Resolution Radar Satellites," LiveScience.com, April 27, 2023, https://www.livescience.com/planet-earth/rivers-oceans/mind-boggling-array-of-19000-undersea-volcanoes-discovered-with-high-resolution-radar-satellites.

16. Anthony Blair, "CRACK OF DOOM Red Alert for Magnitude-9 Mega-Earthquake off Pacific Coast as Crack Discovered in 600-Mile Fault at Bottom of Ocean," *U.S. Sun*, April 14, 2023, https://www.the-sun.com/tech/7871796/earthquake-pacific-coast-california-oregon-big-one.

17. Jeff Van Hatten, "Prophetical Earthquake Statistics," *The Prophecy Watcher* (May 2022): 40–41.

18. John F. Walvoord, *The Prophecy Knowledge Handbook* (Wheaton, Illinois: Victory Books, 1990), 563–64.

19. Robert Lea, "As Sun's Most Active Regions Turn toward Earth, Potential for Violent Solar Activity Builds," Space.com, January 13, 2023, https://www.space.com/sun-active-regions-turn-facing-earth.

20. Mara Johnson-Groh, "Powerful Eruptions on the Sun Might Trigger Earthquakes," Astronomy.com, July 13, 2020, https://www.astronomy.com/science/powerful-eruptions-on-the-sun-might-trigger-earthquakes.

21. European Space Agency, "30,000 Near-Earth Asteroids Discovered, and Numbers Are Rising," Phys.org, October 13, 2022, https://phys.org/news/2022-10-near-earth-asteroids.html.

22. Ibid.

Chapter Three: Vortex of Evil

1. Matthew Rozsa, "An Extinction-Level Asteroid That Could Someday Hit Earth Was Found Hiding Near Venus," Salon, December 7, 2022, https://www.salon.com/2022/12/07/an-extinction-level-asteroid-that-could-someday-hit-earth-was-found-hiding-near-venus.

2. *Britannica Online*, s.v. "Illuminati," accessed September 4, 2023, https://www.britannica.com/search?query=ILLUMINATI.

3. Devra Newberger Speregen and Debra Mostow Zakarin, *Secret Societies: The Truth Revealed* (Plain City, Ohio: Media Source, 2013), 10.

4. Ibid.

5. Kelly Knauer and *TIME* editors, *TIME Secret Societies: Decoding the Myths and Facts of History's Most Mysterious Organizations* (New York: Time Inc. Home Entertainment, 2010), 26–27.

6. Ibid., 10.

7. Ibid., 26–27.

8. Ibid.

9. Jim Marrs, *The Illuminati: The Secret Society that Hijacked the World* (Detroit: Visible Ink Press, 2017), 90.

10. Ibid., 89–92.

11. Jim Marrs, *Rule by Secrecy: The Hidden History that Connects the Trilateral Commission, the Freemasons, and the Great Pyramids* (New York: HarperCollins Publishers, 2000), 7, 11, 21–110.

12. *Mysteries of History: Secret Societies* (Washington, DC: *U.S. News & World Report*, 2008), 1–57.

13. Jean-Pierre Isbouts, *Secret Societies: True Tales of Covert Cults and Organizations and Their Leaders* (Washington, D.C.: National Geographic, 2017), 5, https://www.amazon.com/National-Geographic-Secret-Societies-Organizations/dp/1683301188.

14. Joe Biden, "Remarks by President Biden before Business Roundtable's CEO Quarterly Meeting," White House, Washington, D.C., March 21, 2022, https://www.whitehouse.gov/briefing-room/speeches-remarks/2022/03/21/remarks-by-president-biden-before-business-roundtables-ceo-quarterly-meeting.

15. Ken Moriyasu and Shigesaburo Okumura, "Trilateral Commission Calls 2023 'Year One' of New World Order," Nikkei Asia, March 14, 2023, https://asia.nikkei.com/Politics/International-relations/Indo-Pacific/Trilateral-Commission-calls-2023-Year-One-of-new-world-order.

16. William F. Jasper, "Intel's Real Target: America," *New American* 39, no. 10 (May 29, 2023), https://thenewamerican.com/print/intels-real-target-america.

17. "Seven Global Conflicts to Watch in 2023," Carnegie Corporation of New York, February 8, 2023, https://www.carnegie.org/our-work/article/seven-global-conflicts-watch-2023.

18. Reuters, "Xi and Putin Pledge to Shape a New World Order as the Chinese Leader Leaves Russia with No Peace in Sight for Ukraine," NBC News, March 22, 2023, https://www.nbcnews.com/news/world/xi-putin-pledge-new-world-order-chinese-leader-leaves-russia-rcna76048.

19. Charlie Campbell, "China Just Brokered a Historic Truce between Saudi Arabia and Iran. Can It Do Ukraine Next?," *TIME*, March 15, 2023, https://time.com/6262985/china-saudi-arabia-iran-ukraine-peace-talks.

20. Tim LaHaye and Ed Hindson, *The Popular Encyclopedia of Bible Prophecy* (Eugene, Oregon: Harvest House Publishers, 2004), 119–22.

21. Gerald M. Feierstein and Yoel Guzansky, "Two Years On, What Is the State of the Abraham Accords?," Middle East Institute, September 14, 2022, https://www.mei.edu/publications/two-years-what-state-abraham-accords.

22. Paul Begley, "The Final Peace Deal Middle East / Irvin Baxter / Paul Begley," YouTube, 28:24, September 29, 2018, https://www.youtube.com/watch?v=NslqDiufN4Q.

23. The CRC maintains a list of results from its ongoing research in the American Worldview Inventory, which can be accessed at https://www.arizonachristian.edu/culturalresearchcenter/research.

24. Tracy Munsil, "US Moral Freefall—Survey Finds America's Traditional Moral Pillars Are Fading Away," Cultural Research Center, Arizona Christian University, June 2, 2020, https://www.arizonachristian.edu/2020/06/02/us-moral-freefall-survey-finds-americas-traditional-moral-pillars-are-fading-away.

25. Antonio Pagliarulo, "Why Paganism and Witchcraft Are Making a Comeback," Think, October 30, 2022, https://www.nbcnews.com/think/opinion/paganism-witchcraft-are-making-comback-rcna54444.

26. Jamie Wilde, "The Occult Is Having a Moment," Morning Brew, October 29, 2021, https://www.morningbrew.com/daily/stories/2021/10/29/the-occult-is-having-a-moment.

27. Jeannie Ortega Law, "Christians Share Jesus with Satanists at Boston SatanCon: 'We Showed Them Kindness, Love in the Name of Jesus,'"

Christian Post, May 3, 2023, https://www.christianpost.com/news/christians
-share-jesus-with-satanists-at-boston-satancon.html.

28. Geoffrey Grider, "Monster Energy Drink Company Launches 'The Beast
Unleashed' Hard Seltzer Alcoholic Beverage Complete with 666 and the All-
Seeing Eye on Every Can," Now The End Begins, March 14, 2023, https://
www.nowtheendbegins.com/monster-energy-drink-company-launches-beast
-unleashed-666-satanism-antichrist.

29. Jack Seale, "Little Demon Review—Danny DeVito's Super-Fun Animation
Is Absolute Filth," *The Guardian*, January 18, 2023, https://www
.theguardian.com/tv-and-radio/2023/jan/18/little-demon-review-danny
-devitos-super-fun-animation-is-absolute-filth.

30. Anna Tong, "AI Threatens Humanity's Future, 61% of Americans Say:
Reuters/Ipsos Poll," Reuters, updated May 17, 2023, https://www.reuters
.com/technology/ai-threatens-humanitys-future-61-americans-say
-reutersipsos-2023-05-17.

31. Eliezer Yudkowsky, "Pausing AI Developments Isn't Enough. We Need to
Shut It All Down," *TIME*, March 29, 2023, https://time.com/6266923/ai
-eliezer-yudkowsky-open-letter-not-enough.

32. Gregory Wallace, "Elon Musk Warns against Unleashing Artificial
Intelligence 'Demon,'" CNN Business, October 26, 2014, https://money.cnn
.com/2014/10/26/technology/elon-musk-artificial-intelligence-demon.

33. Thomas R. Horn et al., *The Milieu: Welcome to the Transhuman Resistance*
(Crane, Missouri: Defender Publishing, 2018), 175–76.

34. Fiona Macdonald, "Theoretical Physicists Suggest There's a Portal Linking
the Standard Model to Dark Physics," GE, March 26, 2017, https://www.ge
.com/news/reports/theoretical-physicists-suggest-theres-portal-linking
-standard-model-dark-physics.

35. Ibid.

36. Cathal Kelly, "Collider Could Open Hole to New Dimensions," *Toronto
Star*, November 9, 2009, https://www.thestar.com/business/tech_news/2009
/11/09/collider_could_open_hole_to_new_dimensions.html.

37. "Lord Shiva Statue Unveiled," CERN, July 5, 2004, https://cds.cern.ch/
record/745737?ln=en.

38. Thomas R. Horn and Josh Peck, *Abaddon Ascending: The Ancient
Conspiracy at the Center of CERN's Most Secretive Mission* (Crane,
Missouri: Defender Publishing, 2016), 48–93.

39. Douglas Woodward, interview by Troy Anderson, January 18, 2022.

40. Paul Begley, "ConCERNed about CERN," webcast on Paul Begley Prophecy, https://www.paulbegleyprophecy.com/cern2023.

41. Thomas R. Horn, *Zeitgeist 2025: Countdown to the Secret Destiny of America* (Crane, Missouri: Defender Publishing, 2021), 20–21.

Chapter Four: At the Crossroads

1. Dennis Pamlin and Stuart Armstrong, *Global Challenges: 12 Risks That Threaten Human Civilisation*, Global Challenges Foundation, February 2015, https://static1.squarespace.com/static/59dc930532601e9d148e3c25/t/5 abf5a638a922d9f4625aff9/1522489978866/12+Risks+with+infinite+impact-Executive+Summary.pdf.

2. Klaus Schwab, "Now Is the Time for a 'Great Reset,'" World Economic Forum, June 3, 2020, https://www.weforum.org/agenda/2020/06/now-is-the-time-for-a-great-reset.

3. Klaus Schwab and Thierry Malleret, *COVID-19: The Great Reset* (Geneva, Switzerland: World Economic Forum, 2020), 11–12.

4. Chloe Taylor, "Coronavirus Crisis Presents a 'Golden Opportunity' to Reboot the Economy, Prince Charles Says," CNBC, June 3, 2020, https://www.cnbc.com/2020/06/03/prince-charles-covid-19-a-golden-opportunity-to-reboot-the-economy.html.

5. Alex Newman, "Great Reset: Happening Now," *New American* 38, no. 21 (Novermber 14, 2022), https://thenewamerican.com/print/great-reset-happening-now.

6. World Economic Forum, "8 Predictions for the World in 2030," Facebook, November 18, 2016, https://www.facebook.com/watch/?v=10153920 524981479.

7. Lucy Pérez et al., "Does ESG Really Matter—and Why?," *McKinsey Quarterly*, August 10, 2022, https://www.mckinsey.com/capabilities/sustainability/our-insights/does-esg-really-matter-and-why.

8. Billy Crone, *The Great Covid Deception* (Las Vegas: Get a Life Ministries, 2022), 21–23.

9. Ibid.

10. Ibid.

11. Elizabeth Schulze, "Everything You Need to Know about the Fourth Industrial Revolution," CNBC, updated January 22, 2019, https://www.cnbc.com/2019/01/16/fourth-industrial-revolution-explained-davos-2019.html.

12. Klaus Schwab, quoted in Elizabeth Schulze, "Everything You Need to Know about the Fourth Industrial Revolution," CNBC, updated January 22, 2019,

https://www.cnbc.com/2019/01/16/fourth-industrial-revolution-explained
-davos-2019.html.

13. Billy Crone, interview by Troy Anderson, April 12, 2022.

14. "Modeling the Future of Religion in America," Pew Research Center, September 13, 2022, https://www.pewresearch.org/religion/2022/09/13/modeling-the-future-of-religion-in-america.

15. Battle Ready Ministries, "Letter to the American Church with Eric Metaxas (Pt. 1) FrontLine: Battle Ready Ministries (#41)," YouTube video, 29:23, February 13, 2023, https://www.youtube.com/watch?v=NImaKAMJtSE&t=120s.

16. Battle Ready Ministries, "Letter to the American Church with Eric Metaxas (Pt. 2) FrontLine: Battle Ready Ministries (#42)," YouTube, 25:44, February 20, 2023, https://www.youtube.com/watch?v=1em3TuaUjYk&t=6s.

17. Ibid.

18. *Britannica Online*, s.v. "Final Solution," accessed June 26, 2023, https://www.britannica.com/event/Final-Solution.

19. "'Jewish Assets Seized by Nazis Funded 30 Percent of WWII Expenses,'" *Haaretz*, November 8, 2010, https://www.haaretz.com/jewish/2010-11-08/ty-article/jewish-assets-seized-by-nazis-funded-30-percent-of-wwii-expenses/0000017f-eb70-d0f7-a9ff-eff5ca250000.

20. Dan McLaughlin, "Joe Biden's Blundering, Insincere Philadelphia Speech," *National Review*, September 2, 2022, https://www.nationalreview.com/corner/joe-bidens-blundering-insincere-philadelphia-speech.

21. Jeffrey M. Jones, "Social Conservatism in U.S. Highest in About a Decade," Gallup, June 8, 2023, https://news.gallup.com/poll/506765/social-conservatism-highest-decade.aspx.

22. Joe Biden, "Remarks by President Biden on the Continued Battle for the Soul of the Nation," White House, Philadelphia, September 1, 2022, https://www.whitehouse.gov/briefing-room/speeches-remarks/2022/09/01/remarks-by-president-bidenon-the-continued-battle-for-the-soul-of-the-nation.

23. Church International, "Rosh Hashanah Sunday Evening Service 9/17/2023," YouTube, 2:34:49, September 17, 2023, https://www.youtube.com/watch?v=j9VVsVAoOnc.

24. European Union, "AI Can Write a New Bible," Christian Network Europe, June 16, 2023, https://cne.news/article/3207-ai-can-write-a-new-bible.

25. r/Damnthatsinteresting, "Yuval Noah Harari: 'We Will Be beyond the God of the Bible,'" Reddit, 2022, https://www.reddit.com/r/Damnthatsinteresting/comments/xarrhv/yuval_noah_harari_we_will_be_beyond_the_god_of.

26. "The Declaration of Independence," America's Founding Documents, National Archives, accessed November 7, 2023, https://www.archives.gov/founding-docs/declaration.

27. "First Amendment," Constitution of the United States, Congress.gov, https://constitution.congress.gov/constitution/amendment-1.

28. *Merriam-Webster Dictionary*, s.v. "wile," accessed November 7, 2023, https://www.merriam-webster.com/dictionary/wile.

29. Mitchell Landsberg, "Evangelical Leaders Echo Obama, Say U.S. Not a Christian Nation," *Los Angeles Times*, July 31, 2012, https://www.latimes.com/politics/la-xpm-2012-jul-31-la-pn-evangelical-leaders-echo-obama-say-us-not-a-christian-nation-20120731-story.html.

30. Tracy Munsil, "Biblical Worldview among U.S. Adults Drops 33% Since Start of COVID-19 Pandemic," Arizona Christian University Cultural Research Center, February 28, 2023, https://www.arizonachristian.edu/2023/02/28/biblical-worldview-among-u-s-adults-drops-33-since-start-of-covid-19-pandemic.

31. George Barna, "Release #6: What Does It Mean When People Say They Are 'Christian'?," *American Worldview Inventory #1*, Arizona Christian University Cultural Research Center, August 31, 2021, https://www.arizonachristian.edu/wp-content/uploads/2021/08/CRC_AWVI2021_Release06_Digital_01_20210831.pdf.

32. Ibid.

33. Ibid.

34. John McLaughlin and Jim McLaughlin, "McLaughlin Poll: Trump Beats Biden in Electoral Landslide," Newsmax, August 29, 2023, https://www.newsmax.com/mclaughlin/biden-fulton-trump/2023/08/29/id/1132479.

35. MyFaithVotes.org, homepage, https://www.myfaithvotes.org.

36. Elizabeth Dias, "The Evangelical Fight to Win Back California," *New York Times*, May 27, 2018, https://www.nytimes.com/2018/05/27/us/politics/franklin-graham-evangelicals-california.html.

37. Battle Ready Ministries, "Revival Unleashed: Pastor Todd Coconato's Game-Changing Insights!," YouTube, 24:05, June 16, 2023, https://www.youtube.com/watch?v=4OpB3FuO9WE&t=438s.

Chapter Five: The Great Reset

1. Yuval Noah Harari, *Homo Deus: A Brief History of Tomorrow* (New York: Harper Perennial, 2017), 34–35.

2. Arion McNicoll, "How Google's Calico Aims to Fight Aging and 'Solve Death,'" CNN, updated October 3, 2013, https://www.cnn.com/2013/10/03/tech/innovation/google-calico-aging-death/index.html.

3. Katrina Brooker, "Google Ventures and the Search for Immortality," Bloomberg, March 8, 2015, https://www.bloomberg.com/news/articles/2015-03-09/google-ventures-bill-maris-investing-in-idea-of-living-to-500?embedded-checkout=true.

4. Harari, *Homo Deus*, 25.

5. *Britannica Online*, s.v. "transhumanism," accessed September 5, 2023, https://www.britannica.com/topic/transhumanism.

6. Yuval Noah Harari, "The Last Days of Death," *Open*, September 8, 2016, https://openthemagazine.com/essay/the-last-days-of-death.

7. Harari, *Homo Deus*, 44.

8. Ibid, 44–45.

9. "British Microchip Implant Takes Hand-Swipe Payments to Next Level, Along with End Times Prophecy Concerns," CBN, May 12, 2022, https://www2.cbn.com/news/world/british-microchip-implant-takes-hand-swipe-payments-next-level-along-end-times-prophecy.

10. Steve Warren, "Would You Like a Microchip in Your Brain? Vast Majority Worry about Totalitarian Control as Tech Advances," CBN, January 26, 2022, https://www2.cbn.com/news/us/would-you-microchip-your-brain-vast-majority-worry-about-totalitarian-control-tech-advances.

11. Jeremy Zogby, "Human vs. Human 2.0; 10% Welcome Microchip in Brain—Nearly 80% Worry about It," John Zogby Strategies, January 24, 2022, https://johnzogbystrategies.com/human-vs-human-2-0-10-welcome-microchip-in-brain-nearly-80-worry-about-it.

12. Kevin Jessip and Troy Anderson, "Is the False Prophet Alive and Well on Planet Earth?," Charisma News, July 7, 2022, https://www.charismanews.com/opinion/89615-is-the-false-prophet-alive-and-well-on-planet-earth.

13. "The SDGS in Action," United Nations, https://www.undp.org/sustainable-development-goals.

14. UN Development Programme, "5 Things You Need to Know about the 2030 Agenda for Sustainable Development," Medium, December 3, 2018, https://undp.medium.com/5-things-you-need-to-know-about-the-2030-agenda-for-sustainable-development-380405b44e3c.

15. Jessilyn Lancaster, "Bible Prophecy Experts Share What You Need to Know about UN's Agenda 2030," Charisma News, September 18, 2015, https://

www.charismanews.com/opinion/52300-bible-prophecy-experts-share-what
-you-need-to-know-about-un-s-agenda-2030.

16. Michael Snyder, "Did the United Nations Just Introduce a New World
Order?," Charisma News, September 30, 2015, https://www.charismanews
.com/opinion/52333-did-the-united-nations-just-introduce-a-new-world
-order.

17. Sarah Repucci and Amy Slipowitz, "Freedom in the World 2022: The Global
Expansion of Authoritarian Rule," Freedom House, 2022, https://
freedomhouse.org/report/freedom-world/2022/global-expansion
-authoritarian-rule.

18. Archbishop Carlo Maria Viganò, "New from Archbishop Viganò: The Great
Reset from Start to Finish," LifeSiteNews.com, March 31, 2021, https://www
.lifesitenews.com/opinion/new-from-archbishop-vigano-the-great-reset-from
-start-to-finish.

19. Glenn Beck, *The Great Reset: Joe Biden and the Rise of the 21st Century
Fascism* (Irving, Texas: Mercury Ink, 2022), front cover.

20. Klaus Schwab and Thierry Malleret, *The Great Narrative for a Better Future*
(Geneva, Switzerland: World Economic Forum, 2022), 12–27.

21. Jan Hatzius et al., "The Potentially Large Effects of Artificial Intelligence on
Economic Growth (Briggs/Kodnani)," Goldman Sachs, March 26, 2023,
https://www.key4biz.it/wp-content/uploads/2023/03/Global-Economics
-Analyst_-The-Potentially-Large-Effects-of-Artificial-Intelligence-on
-Economic-Growth-Briggs_Kodnani.pdf.

22. Alice Bailey, *The Externalisation of the Hierarchy* (New York: Lucis Trust,
1957), 485–86; Lucis Trust, "Support of the United Nations," https://www
.lucistrust.org/about_us/support_un; Lucis Trust, "About Us," https://www
.lucistrust.org/about_us/history.

23. "The President and the Press: Address Before the American Newspaper
Publishers Association, April 27, 1961," John F. Kennedy Presidential Library
and Museum, April 27, 1961, https://www.jfklibrary.org/archives/other
-resources/john-f-kennedy-speeches/american-newspaper-publishers
-association-19610427.

24. Jim Marrs, *The Illuminati: The Secret Society that Hijacked the World*
(Detroit: Visible Ink Press, 2017), xviii.

25. Aryn Baker, "They're Healthy. They're Sustainable. So Why Don't Humans
Eat More Bugs?," *TIME*, February 26, 2021, https://time.com/5942290/eat
-insects-save-planet.

26. Matthew Smith, "One in Five Americans Say They're Willing to Eat Insects," YouGov.com, November 5, 2021, https://today.yougov.com/topics/international/articles-reports/2021/11/05/one-five-americans-say-theyre-willing-eat-insects.

27. Mary Walrath-Holdridge, "Lab-Grown Chicken, Meat Could Soon Find Its Way onto American Plates after USDA Approval," *USA Today*, July 6, 2023, https://www.usatoday.com/story/money/2023/07/06/lab-grown-meat-chicken-approval-us/70388000007.

28. Geoffrey Grider, "AGENDA 2030: The USDA Approves Bill Gates Lab-Grown 'Frankenfood' Meat as Our Global Society Lurches Ever Forward into a Dystopian Abyss," NowTheEndBegins.com, July 12, 2023, https://www.nowtheendbegins.com/usda-approves-agenda-2030-bill-gates-frankenfood-cultivated-lab-grown-meat.

29. Amy Quinton, "Lab-Grown Meat's Carbon Footprint Potentially Worse Than Retail Beef," University of California, Davis, May 22, 2023, https://www.ucdavis.edu/food/news/lab-grown-meat-carbon-footprint-worse-beef.

30. Lizzie O'Leary, "Lab-Grown Meat Is Full of Contradictions (and Other Things, Too)," Slate, December 21, 2022, https://slate.com/technology/2022/12/lab-grown-meat-problem-raw-deal.html.

31. Jane M. Caldwell, "What's All the Buzz about Edible Insects?," Institute of Food Technologies, May 1, 2022, https://www.ift.org/news-and-publications/food-technology-magazine/issues/2022/may/columns/safety-and-quality-edible-insects.

32. Dave Hunt, *A Woman Rides the Beast* (Eugene, Oregon: Harvest House Publishers, 1994), 43–45.

33. Jonathan Franzen, "What If We Stopped Pretending?," *New Yorker*, September 8, 2019, https://www.newyorker.com/culture/cultural-comment/what-if-we-stopped-pretending.

34. David Guzik, *Revelation: Verse by Verse Commentary* (Goleta, California: Enduring Word, 2019), 211–14.

35. Ibid.

Chapter Six: The Green Religion

1. "The Global Religious Landscape," Pew Research Center, December 18, 2012, https://www.pewresearch.org/religion/2012/12/18/global-religious-landscape-exec.

2. *Britannica Online*, s.v. "Gaia hypothesis," accessed July 15, 2023, https:// www.britannica.com/science/Gaia-hypothesis.

3. Richard O' Leary, *The Environmental Mafia: The Enemy Is Us* (New York: Algora Publishing, 2003), 27.

4. Samantha Smith, *Goddess Earth: Exposing the Pagan Agenda of the Environmental Movement* (Lafayette, Louisiana: Huntington House Publishers, 1994), 10–11.

5. James E. Lovelock, "James Lovelock: The Earth Is about to Catch a Morbid Fever That May Last as Long as 100,000 Years," *The Independent*, January 16, 2006, https://web.archive.org/web/20060408121826/http://comment .independent.co.uk/commentators/article338830.ece.

6. "'Gaia' scientist James Lovelock: I Was 'Alarmist' about Climate Change," NBCNews.com, April 23, 2012, https://www.nbcnews.com/news/world/ gaia-scientist-james-lovelock-i-was-alarmist-about-climate-change -flna730066.

7. "What Is Climate Change?," NASA, https://climate.nasa.gov/global-warming -vs-climate-change.

8. William Cummings, "'The World Is Going to End in 12 Years If We Don't Address Climate Change,' Ocasio-Cortez Says," *USA Today*, January 22, 2019, https://www.usatoday.com/story/news/politics/onpolitics/2019/01/22/ ocasio-cortez-climate-change-alarm/2642481002.

9. "Secretary-General Warns of Climate Emergency, Calling Intergovernmental Panel's Report 'a File of Shame' While Saying Leaders 'Are Lying,' Fuelling Flames," United Nations, April 4, 2022, https://press.un.org/en/2022/ sgsm21228.doc.htm.

10. "What Is Climate Change?"

11. Ibid.

12. "World Climate Declaration: There Is No Climate Emergency," Global Climate Intelligence Group, August 14, 2023, https://heartland.org/wp -content/uploads/2023/08/WorldClimate-Declaration-There-Is-No-Climate -Emergency-CLINTEL-August-14-2023.pdf.

13. Ibid.

14. Alex Newman, "The UN's New World Religion," *New American* 39, no. 1 (January 16, 2023), https://thenewamerican.com/print/the-uns-new-world -religion.

15. "COP27: Archbishop of Canterbury Says World 'Near Point of No Return' and Calls for Climate Justice," Archbishop of Canterbury, May 11, 2022, https://www.archbishopofcanterbury.org/news/news-and-statements/

cop27-archbishop-canterbury-says-world-near-point-no-return-and-calls
#:~:text=%22The%20climate%20emergency%20is%20an,damage
%20caused%20by%20climate%20change.

16. Billy Crone, telephone interview by Troy Anderson, March 7, 2017.

17. *Britannica Online*, s.v. "New Age movement," accessed September 9, 2023, https://www.britannica.com/topic/New-Age-movement.

18. Ibid.

19. George Barna, "Release #6: What Does It Mean When People Say They Are 'Christian'?," Arizona Christian University Cultural Research Center, August 31, 2021, https://www.arizonachristian.edu/wp-content/uploads/2021/08/CRC_AWVI2021_Release06_Digital_01_20210831.pdf.

20. Crone, telephone interview.

21. Ibid.

22. *Britannica Online*, s.v. "Thomas Malthus," accessed July 17, 2023, https://www.britannica.com/biography/Thomas-Malthus.

23. Charles C. Mann, "The Book That Incited a Worldwide Fear of Overpopulation," *Smithsonian Magazine* (January 2018), https://www.smithsonianmag.com/innovation/book-incited-worldwide-fear-overpopulation-180967499.

24. Mark J. Perry, "18 Spectacularly Wrong Predictions Made around the Time of the First Earth Day in 1970, Expect More This Year," American Enterprise Institute, April 21, 2016, https://www.aei.org/carpe-diem/18-spectacularly-wrong-apocalyptic-predictions-made-around-the-time-of-the-first-earth-day-in-1970-expect-more-this-year-3.

25. Mann, "The Book That Incited a Worldwide Fear of Overpopulation."

26. Jim Marrs, *Population Control: How Corporate Owners Are Killing Us* (New York: William Morrow, 2015), book cover, 1–4.

27. Jada White, "Georgia Guidestones: Mystery Surrounding Explosion Remains a Year Later," Fox 5 Atlanta, July 5, 2023, https://www.fox5atlanta.com/news/mystery-surrounding-georgia-guidestones-explosion-remains-a-year-later.

28. Bernie Sanders, "The Rich-Poor Gap in America Is Obscene. So Let's Fix It—Here's How," *The Guardian*, March 29, 2021, https://www.theguardian.com/commentisfree/2021/mar/29/rich-poor-gap-wealth-inequality-bernie-sanders.

29. Marrs, *Population Control*, 1–4.

30. Staff, "Malone: CIA and the Covid Pandemic," *New American* 39, no. 17 (September 11, 2023), https://thenewamerican.com/print/malone-cia-and-the -covid-pandemic.

31. "National Security Study Memorandum (NSSM 200): Implications of Worldwide Population Growth for U.S. Security and Overseas Interests (THE KISSINGER REPORT)," National Security Council, December 10, 1974, https://pdf.usaid.gov/pdf_docs/Pcaab500.pdf.

32. "World Population Prospects 2022," United Nations Department of Economic and Social Affairs, Population Division, 2022, https://www.un .org/development/desa/pd/sites/www.un.org.development.desa.pd/files/ wpp2022_summary_of_results.pdf.

33. "Child Mortality (Under 5 Years)," World Health Organization, January 28, 2022, https://www.who.int/news-room/fact-sheets/detail/levels-and-trends -in-child-under-5-mortality-in-2020; Max Roser, "Extreme Poverty: How Far Have We Come, and How Far Do We Still Have to Go?," Our World in Data, August 27, 2023, https://ourworldindata.org/extreme-poverty-in-brief; Tony Morley, "9 Astonishing Ways That Living Standards Have Improved around the World," Big Think, October 14, 2022, https://bigthink.com/the -present/9-ways-living-standards-improved-world.

34. Marian L. Tupy and Gale L. Pooley, "Superabundance," Cato Institute, August 2022, https://www.cato.org/books/superabundance.

35. "About Us," Mensa International, https://www.mensa.org/mensa/about-us.

36. "WHO Coronavirus (COVID-19) Dashboard," World Health Organization, https://covid19.who.int/?mapFilter=deaths.

37. Nick Koutsobinas, "Medical Journal: 17M Excess Deaths Due to COVID-19," Newsmax, September 26, 2022, https://www.newsmax.com/newsfront /covid-19-excess-deaths-vaccines/2022/09/26/id/1089153.

38. "'Died Suddenly'? More Than 1-in-4 Think Someone They Know Died from COVID-19 Vaccines," Rasmussen Reports, January 2, 2023, https://www .rasmussenreports.com/public_content/politics/public_surveys/died_ suddenly_more_than_1_in_4_think_someone_they_know_died_from _covid_19_vaccines.

39. Paul Begley, *Mark of the Beast, RFID* (San Francisco: Blurb, 2012), 29–30.

40. Ibid., 36–51.

41. Emily Mangiaracina, "Top Economist: Central Bankers Are Planning CBDC Currency Implants 'Under Your Skin,'" LifeSiteNews.com, July 12, 2023, https://www.lifesitenews.com/news/top-economist-central-bankers-are -planning-cbdc-currency-implants-under-your-skin.

42. Ibid.
43. Kristalina Georgieva, "The Future of Money: Gearing Up for Central Bank Digital Currency," International Monetary Fund, February 9, 2022, https://www.imf.org/en/News/Articles/2022/02/09/sp020922-the-future-of-money-gearing-up-for-central-bank-digital-currency.
44. Ibid.
45. Paul Begley, "Prophecy Alert: 'The Mark of the Beast' 666 Irvin Baxter & Paul Begley," YouTube, October 12, 2018, https://youtu.be/rdQobx9Unno?si=iogXq3eTjVVmGwKF.
46. Ibid.

Chapter Seven: Family, Woke Education, and Cultural Marxism

1. *Britannica Online*, s.v. "Frankfurt School" accessed July 20, 2023, https://www.britannica.com/topic/Frankfurt-School.
2. Alex Newman, "Frankfurt School Weaponized US Education against Civilization," *Epoch Times*, November 5, 2019, https://www.theepochtimes.com/opinion/frankfurt-school-weaponized-u-s-education-against-civilization-3137064.
3. Ibid.
4. *Britannica Online*, s.v. "Herbert Marcuse," accessed July 21, 2023, https://www.britannica.com/biography/Herbert-Marcuse.
5. Mike Gonzalez and Katharine Gorka, "How Cultural Marxism Threatens the United States—and How Americans Can Fight It," Heritage Foundation, November 14, 2022, https://www.heritage.org/progressivism/report/how-cultural-marxism-threatens-the-united-states-and-how-americans-can-fight.
6. Ibid.
7. W. Cleon Skousen, *The Naked Communist: Exposing Communism and Restoring Freedom* (Salt Lake City, Utah: Izzard Ink Publishing Company, 2017), 299–328.
8. Paul McGuire, telephone interview by Troy Anderson, May 29, 2021.
9. "Modest Declines in Positive Views of 'Socialism' and 'Capitalism' in U.S.," Pew Research Center, September 19, 2022, https://www.pewresearch.org/politics/2022/09/19/modest-declines-in-positive-views-of-socialism-and-capitalism-in-u-s.
10. Bill Chappell, "Supreme Court Declares Same-Sex Marriage Legal in All 50 States," NPR, June 26, 2015, https://www.npr.org/sections/thetwo-way/2015/06/26/417717613/supreme-court-rules-all-states-must-allow-same-sex-marriages.

11. Conor Murray, "Definitive Guide to the Anti-'Woke' Protests: From Bud Light to Target to the U.S. Navy—and Everyone Else," *Forbes*, June 21, 2023, https://www.forbes.com/sites/conormurray/2023/05/20/far-right-pundits-are -slamming-companies-including-nike-adidas-and-ford-for-lgbtq-outreach-as -pride-month-nears/?sh=2dfef5b976d0.

12. Tim LaHaye and Ed Hindson, *The Popular Encyclopedia of Bible Prophecy* (Eugene, Oregon: Harvest House Publishers, 2004), 206–207.

13. "'Transgenderism' Brings Chaos from Order," Focus on the Family, September 13, 2015, https://www.focusonthefamily.com/get-help/ transgenderism-brings-chaos-from-order.

14. Sara Moniuszko, "Teen Mental Health Is in Crisis, Study Shows. What Can Parents Do?," CBS News, March 6, 2023, https://www.cbsnews.com/news /teen-mental-health-crisis-what-can-parents-do.

15. Ibid.

16. Susan Miller, "Gen Z Is Driving Force among Adults Identifying as LGBTQ, Poll Shows. Here's a Breakdown," *USA Today*, February 22, 2023, https:// www.usatoday.com/story/news/nation/2023/02/22/gallup-poll-lgbtq -identification/11309075002.

17. Lucas Miles, interview by Colonel David J. Giammona and Troy Anderson, May 22, 2023, National Religious Broadcasters Convention.

18. Ibid.

19. Amanda Barroso, "More Than Half of Americans Say Marriage Is Important but Not Essential to Leading a Fulfilling Life," Pew Research Center, February 14, 2020, https://www.pewresearch.org/short-reads/2020/02/14/ more-than-half-of-americans-say-marriage-is-important-but-not-essential -to-leading-a-fulfilling-life.

20. Battle Ready Ministries, "Spiritual Sickness Exposed: Pastor Robert Jeffress Unveils the Cure!," YouTube, 17:47, June 29, 2023, https://www.youtube .com/watch?v=ALnh6BvTLuA&t=937s.

21. Ibid.

22. George Barna, "American Worldview Inventory 2022: Release #3: A Detailed Look at How the Worldview of Parents of Preteens Misses the Mark," Arizona Christian University Cultural Research Center, April 12, 2022, https://www.arizonachristian.edu/wp-content/uploads/2022/04/AWVI2022 _Release_03_DigitalVersion.pdf.

23. Ibid.

24. Ibid.

Chapter Eight: Breaking the Seals

1. Henry H. Halley, *Halley's Bible Handbook*, 25th ed. (Grand Rapids: Zondervan, 2007), 827–35.
2. *Britannica Online*, s.v. "St. John the Apostle," accessed September 10, 2023, https://www.britannica.com/biography/Saint-John-the-Apostle.
3. Ibid.
4. F. Kenton Beshore, *Revelation: God's Greatest Triumph* (Costa Mesa, California: World Bible Society, 2016), 21.
5. Mariners Church, "Start with the Ending | The Best is Yet To Come—Eric Geiger," YouTube, January 9, 2022, https://www.youtube.com/watch?v=PjTmd5WTumA.
6. David R. Reagan, "50 Reasons Why We Are Living in the End Times," Lamb and Lion Ministries, https://christinprophecy.org/articles/50-reasons.
7. Pastor Greg Laurie, "An Invasion of Demons Is Coming in the Last Days (Prophecy Points)," YouTube, March 3, 2022, https://www.youtube.com/watch?v=jzgYauFq60M&t=4s.
8. Tim LaHaye and Timothy E. Parker, *The Book of Revelation Made Clear* (Nashville, Tennessee: Thomas Nelson, 2014), 43.
9. Halley, *Halley's Bible Handbook*, 851.
10. Tim LaHaye, telephone interview by Troy Anderson, August 29, 2014.
11. David Guzik, *Revelation: Verse by Verse Commentary* (Goleta, California: Enduring Word, 2019), 102; Halley, *Halley's Bible Handbook*, 853.
12. John F. Walvoord, *The Prophecy Knowledge Handbook* (Wheaton, Illinois: Victory Books, 1990), 552.
13. Toby Ord and Angus Mercer, "Politicians Need to Pay Attention to Existential Risks," *Wired*, August 21, 2021, https://www.wired.co.uk/article/existential-risk-catastrophe-future-proof.
14. "World Military Expenditure Reaches New Record High as European Spending Surges," Stockholm International Peace Research Institute, April 24, 2023, https://www.sipri.org/media/press-release/2023/world-military-expenditure-reaches-new-record-high-european-spending-surges.
15. Dr. F. Kenton Beshore, *Revelation: God's Greatest Triumph* (Costa Mesa, California: World Bible Society, 2016), 174.

Chapter Nine: The Great North American Eclipse, Apophis, and Planet X

1. Bill Koenig, "The Biblical Significance of the August 21, 2017 and April 8, 2024 Total Solar Eclipses, and the Warnings of Coronavirus, War,

Earthquakes and Famine," Koenig World Watch Daily, May 24, 2023, https://watch.org/node/62147; Rabbi Benjamin Blech, "The Next Solar Eclipse in 2024: A Startling Message for the World," Aish, https://aish.com/the-next-solar-eclipse-in-2024-a-startling-message-for-the-world.

2. Koenig, "The Biblical Significance of the August 21, 2017, and April 8, 2024, Total Solar Eclipses."

3. "Hypothetical Planet X," NASA, https://solarsystem.nasa.gov/planets/hypothetical-planet-x/in-depth.

4. "Apophis: The Asteroid We Thought Might Hit Us in 2029," Physics-Astronomy.com, December 3, 2022, https://www.physics-astronomy.com/apophis-the-asteroid-we-thought-might-hit-us-in-2029.

5. Ian J. O'Neill and Joshua Handal, "NASA Analysis: Earth Is Safe from Asteroid Apophis for 100-Plus Years," NASA, March 26, 2021, https://www.nasa.gov/feature/jpl/nasa-analysis-earth-is-safe-from-asteroid-apophis-for-100-plus-years.

6. Ibid.

7. Robert Lea, "Apophis: The Infamous Asteroid We Thought Might Hit Us," Space.com, December 14, 2022, https://www.space.com/apophis.

8. "The FP Top 100 Global Thinkers," *Foreign Policy*, December 2010, https://web.archive.org/web/20110308081012/http://www.foreignpolicy.com/articles/2010/11/29/the_fp_top_100_global_thinkers?page=0,37.

9. Nathan Myhrvold, "An Empirical Examination of WISE/NEOWISE Asteroid Analysis and Results," *Icarus* 314 (November 2018): 64–97, https://doi.org/10.1016/j.icarus.2018.05.004.

10. Michael Horn, "Open Letter to President Trump," February 15, 2018, They Fly Blog & News, https://theyflyblog.com/2018/02/open-letter-to-president-trump.

11. "Apophis," NASA, September 27, 2022, https://solarsystem.nasa.gov/asteroids-comets-and-meteors/asteroids/apophis/in-depth.

12. *Britannica Online*, s.v. "Percival Lowell," accessed August 2, 2023, https://www.britannica.com/biography/Percival-Lowell.

13. Nadia Drake, "Planet 9 May Be Closer and Easier to Find Than Thought—If It Exists," *National Geographic*, August 31, 2021, https://www.nationalgeographic.com/science/article/planet-9-may-be-closer-and-easier-to-find-than-thought-if-it-exists.

14. "Hypothetical Planet X."

15. Paul Begley, "Breaking: 'Massive Solar Eruption On SUN' / Gill Broussard / Planet X," YouTube, April 10, 2023, https://www.youtube.com/watch?v=9Wemwa2ZlNo.

16. Ibid.

17. "Comets in the Bible," *Christianity Today*, December 21, 1973, https://www.christianitytoday.com/ct/1973/december-21/comets-in-bible.html.

18. Tim LaHaye and Ed Hindson, *The Popular Encyclopedia of Bible Prophecy* (Eugene, Oregon: Harvest House Publishers, 2004), 256.

Chapter Ten: Fallen Angels, the Nephilim, Aliens, UFOs, and "The Great Deception"

1. I. D. E. Thomas, *The Omega Conspiracy: Satan's Last Assault on God's Kingdom* (Crane, Missouri: Anomalos Publishing House, 2008), 23–24.

2. Cornerstone Fellowship with Pastor Allen Nolan, "Nephilim Unveiled, Alien Secrets Revealed: Don't Be Deceived Bible Study," YouTube, September 17, 2023, https://www.youtube.com/watch?v=Cyx8ahCQBTc.

3. Thomas, *The Omega Conspiracy*, 24.

4. Richard J. Dewhurst, *The Ancient Giants Who Ruled America: The Missing Skeletons and the Great Smithsonian Cover-Up* (Rochester, Vermont: Bear & Company, 2014), back cover.

5. L. A. Marzulli, *On the Trail of the Nephilim: Giant Skeletons & Ancient Megalithic Structures* (Malibu, California: Spiral of Life Publishing, 2013), v, 20, 29–30.

6. L. A. Marzulli, Zoom interview by Troy Anderson, June 19, 2023.

7. Ibid.

8. Casey Luskin, "Every Bit Digital: DNA's Programming Really Bugs Some ID Critics," Discovery Institute, March 29, 2010, https://www.discovery.org/a/14391.

9. Helen Paynter, "A Sadomasochistic and Megalomaniacal God? Response to Richard Dawkins, Chapter 7 of *The God Delusion*," Center for the Study of Bible and Violence, January 2019, https://www.csbvbristol.org.uk/2019/01/24/chapter-7-of-the-god-delusion.

10. "Expelled: No Intelligence Allowed," Movieguide, April 18, 2008, https://www.movieguide.org/reviews/movies/expelled-no-intelligence-allowed.html.

11. Marzulli, Zoom interview.

12. *Britannica Online*, s.v. "Flavius Josephus," accessed August 5, 2023, https://www.britannica.com/biography/Flavius-Josephus.

13. J. R. Cole, "It Ain't Necessarily So: Giants and Biblical Literalism," *Creation/ Evolution Journal* 5, no. 1 (Winter 1985), https://ncse.ngo/it-aint-necessarily -so-giants-and-biblical-literalism.

14. Chris Eberhart, "UFO Whistleblower Testifies His Life Was Threatened over Secret Alien Tech Retrieval," Fox News, July 26, 2023. https://www.foxnews .com/us/ufo-whistleblower-testifies-his-life-was-threatened-to-hush-up-about -secret-alien-tech-retrieval.

15. Fatma Khaled, "Government Concealed 'Huge, Huge' Number of UFOs, Senator Says," *Newsweek*, June 23, 2023, https://www.newsweek.com/ government-concealed-huge-huge-number-ufos-senator-says-1808697.

16. Ibid.

17. SALT, "'100%' Aliens Have Already Arrived—Dr. Garry Nolan & Alex Klokus | SALT iConnections New York," YouTube, May 22, 2023, https:// www.youtube.com/watch?v=e2DqdOw6Uy4.

18. Ibid.

19. Laura Eisenhower, "Aliens Above & Below," interview by Paul Begley, webinar on Paul Begley Prophecy, https://paul-begley-prophecy .mybigcommerce.com/aliens-above-and-below/?fbclid=IwAR07HEk Zlzv3C5_QgQkNDQhtwbw-Y9bTIEiR9DvJ90TpHeZ9WYvKPyJsUPw.

20. Anthony Bond, "President Eisenhower Had Three Secret Meetings with Aliens, Former Pentagon Consultant Claims," *Daily Mail*, February 15, 2012, https://www.dailymail.co.uk/news/article-2100947/Eisenhower-secret -meetings-aliens-pentagon-consultant-claims.html.

21. Dwight D. Eisenhower, "President Dwight D. Eisenhower's Farewell Address (1961)," National Archives, https://www.archives.gov/milestone-documents /president-dwight-d-eisenhowers-farewell-address.

22. Robert Lea, "Area 51: What Is It and What Goes on There?," Space.com, April 11, 2022, https://www.space.com/area-51-what-is-it.

23. Eisenhower, "Aliens Above & Below," interview.

24. Hugh Ross, Zoom interview by Troy Anderson, April 26, 2023.

25. Ibid.

26. Ibid.

27. "If Aliens Can Visit, How Did They Get Here?," ABC News, February 24, 2005, https://abcnews.go.com/Technology/Primetime/story?id=528724& page=1.

28. Jeffrey Kluger, "Anyone Hoping for Aliens to Contact Earth Will Have to Wait Another 400 Years At Least," *TIME*, December 21, 2022, https://time .com/6242921/why-extraterrestrials-havent-contacted-earth.

29. Tracy Munsil, "Biblical Worldview among U.S. Adults Drops 33% Since Start of COVID-19 Pandemic," Arizona Christian University Cultural Research Center, February 28, 2023, https://www.arizonachristian.edu/2023 /02/28/biblical-worldview-among-u-s-adults-drops-33-since-start-of-covid -19-pandemic; Michael Foust, "Barna: Biblical Worldview Held by Only 4% of Adults," Baptist Press, December 2, 2003, https://www.baptistpress.com /resource-library/news/barna-biblical-worldview-held-by-only-4-of-adults.

30. Courtney Kennedy and Arnold Lau, "Most Americans Believe in Intelligent Life beyond Earth; Few See UFOs as a Major National Security Threat," Pew Research Center, June 30, 2021, https://www.pewresearch.org/short -reads/2021/06/30/most-americans-believe-in-intelligent-life-beyond-earth -few-see-ufos-as-a-major-national-security-threat.

31. Hugh Ross, Zoom interview by Troy Anderson, September 20, 2021.

32. Ibid.

33. Ibid.

34. L. A. Marzulli, *UFO Disclosure: The 70-Year Coverup Exposed* (Malibu, California: Spiral of Life Publishing, 2018), 153–54.

Chapter Eleven: "The Destroyer"

1. Pastor Greg Laurie, "An Invasion of Demons Is Coming in the Last Days (Prophecy Points)," YouTube, March 3, 2022, https://www.youtube.com/ watch?v=jzgYauFq60M&t=4s.

2. Derek Gilbert, Zoom interview by Troy Anderson, March 1, 2022.

3. Henry H. Halley, *Halley's Bible Handbook with the New International Version*, 25th ed. (Grand Rapids: Zondervan, 2007), 859.

4. F. Kenton Beshore, *Revelation: God's Greatest Triumph* (Costa Mesa, California: World Bible Society, 2016), 197.

5. Pastor Greg Laurie, "An Invasion of Demons Is Coming in the Last Days (Prophecy Points)."

6. "Explore WWII History," National World War II Museum, https://www. nationalww2museum.org/students-teachers/student-resources/explore -wwii-history.

7. David Guzik, *Revelation: Verse by Verse Commentary* (Goleta, California: Enduring Word, 2019), 141.

8. Mark Hitchcock, *The End* (Carol Stream, Illinois: Tyndale Momentum, 2018), 356.

9. Ibid.

10. Gilbert, Zoom interview.

11. Tim LaHaye and Ed Hindson, *The Popular Encyclopedia of Bible Prophecy* (Eugene, Oregon: Harvest House Publishers, 2004), 394.

12. Gary Stearman, "Revisiting the Tower of Babel," Prophecy Watchers, July 26, 2019, https://prophecywatchers.com/revisiting-the-tower-of-babel.

13. Tom Horn and Terry James, *Antichrist and the Final Solution: The Chronology of the Future Finally Revealed* (Crane, Missouri: Defender, 2020), 230–44.

14. Ibid.

15. Natasha Kirtchuk, "Scientists Working to Resurrect Dinosaurs, Extinct Animals," i24 News, February 10, 2023, https://www.i24news.tv/en/news/international/technology-science/1676021879-scientists-working-to-resurrect-dinosaurs-extinct-animals.

16. Horn and James, *Antichrist and the Final Solution*, 243.

17. Ibid., 244.

18. Ibid.

19. Gilbert, Zoom interview.

20. TOI Staff, "Iran's President Threatens Swift Demise for Israel Should It Attack His Country," *The Times of Israel*, May 3, 2023, https://www.timesofisrael.com/irans-president-threatens-swift-demise-for-israel-should-it-attack-his-country.

21. Paul Begley, "Chuck Missler Interview Part 1 of 4," YouTube, 13:39, October 20, 2015, https://www.youtube.com/watch?v=B6SGnNGD8Mo.

22. Kathleen Magramo et al., "Israel-Hamas War Rages as Outcry Grows over Gaza Crisis," CNN, November 7, 2023, https://www.cnn.com/middleeast/live-news/israel-hamas-war-gaza-news-11-09-23/index.html.

23. Weijia Jiang and Eleanor Watson, "U.S. Navy Sends 4 Destroyers to Alaska Coast after 11 Chinese, Russian Warships Spotted in Nearby Waters," CBS News, August 7, 2023, https://www.cbsnews.com/news/us-navy-destroyers-alaska-coast-11-chinese-russian-warships.

Chapter Twelve: The Third Temple, the Antichrist, and the Second Coming

1. F. Kenton Beshore, *Revelation: God's Greatest Triumph* (Costa Mesa, California: World Bible Society, 2016), 200.

2. Ryan Pitterson, *The Final Nephilim* (New York: Days of Noe Publishing, 2021), 47–54.

3. Bob Smietana, "Pastors: The End of the World Is Complicated," Lifeway Research, April 26, 2016, https://news.lifeway.com/2016/04/26/pastors-the -end-of-the-world-is-complicated.

4. "About the Temple Institute," accessed November 7, 2023, Temple Institute, https://templeinstitute.org/about-us.

5. TOI Staff, "In Modern First, Passover Sacrifice to Take Place in Old City," *The Times of Israel*, April 5, 2017, https://www.timesofisrael.com/in-first -passover-sacrifice-to-take-place-in-old-city.

6. Joshua Hammer, "What Is beneath the Temple Mount?," *Smithsonian Magazine* (April 2011), https://www.smithsonianmag.com/history/what-is -beneath-the-temple-mount-920764.

7. Norman H. Andersson, telephone interview by Troy Anderson, June 7, 2017.

8. Ryan Browne, "Elon Musk Warns A.I. Could Create an 'Immortal Dictator from Which We Can Never Escape,'" CNBC, April 6, 2018, https://www .cnbc.com/2018/04/06/elon-musk-warns-ai-could-create-immortal-dictator -in-documentary.html.

9. *Britannica Online*, s.v. "red heifer," accessed August 13, 2023, https://www .britannica.com/topic/red-heifer.

10. Lisa Loraine Baker, "Do Red Heifers Mean the End Times Are Coming?," Christianity.com, September 22, 2022, https://www.christianity.com/wiki/ end-times/red-heifers-end-times-are-coming.html.

11. Tzvi Joffre, "From Texas to Israel: Red Heifers Needed for Temple Arrive," *The Jerusalem Post*, September 20, 2022, https://www.jpost.com/judaism/ article-717650.

12. CRC Staff, "Vast Majority of Americans Stitch Together Patchwork Worldview of Conflicting Beliefs, Making 'Syncretism' Top Worldview among U.S. Adults," Arizona Christian University Cultural Research Center, April 13, 2021, https://www.arizonachristian.edu/2021/04/13/vast-majority -of-americans-stitch-together-patchwork-worldview-of-conflicting-beliefs -making-syncretism-top-worldview-among-u-s-adults.

13. Ken Ham, "Barna: Most Americans Create a 'Customized Worldview,'" Answers in Genesis, September 22, 2022, https://answersingenesis.org/ worldview/barna-most-americans-create-a-customized-worldview.

14. Tracy Munsil, "AWVI 2020 Survey: 1 in 3 US Adults Embrace Salvation through Jesus; More Believe It Can Be 'Earned,'" Arizona Christian University Cultural Research Center, August 4, 2020, https://www .arizonachristian.edu/2020/08/04/1-in-3-us-adults-embrace-salvation -through-jesus-more-believe-it-can-be-earned.

15. Ibid.

16. Harvest.Church, "'Antichrist, America, and Armageddon' by Greg Laurie," YouTube, August 13, 2023, https://www.youtube.com/watch?v= CfvVyto3VUA.

17. Ibid.

18. Tim LaHaye and Ed Hindson, *The Popular Encyclopedia of Bible Prophecy* (Eugene, Oregon: Harvest House Publishers, 2004), 36.

19. Ibid.

20. Ibid.

Chapter Thirteen: God's Prophetic Timing: What's Next?

1. Private conversation between Jim Bakker and Paul Begley between tapings of segments of this episode of *The Jim Bakker Show*: The Jim Bakker Show, "Why Did Russia Warn Israel Not to Get Involved | Pastor Paul Begley on The Jim Bakker Show," YouTube, March 30, 2022, https://www.youtube.com/watch?v=dMzqS5yOreI.

Conclusion: The "Great Harvest Revival" and You

1. "Event Details," The Return: Washington, D.C., September 2020, https://thereturn.org/thereturn-washingtondc.

2. *Britannica Online*, s.v. "Mayflower Compact," accessed August 17, 2023, https://www.britannica.com/topic/Mayflower-Compact.

3. Brandon Showalter, "'The Renewal' Aims to Restore America's Covenant with God: 'The Greatest Harvest in the History of the World,'" *Christian Post*, December 28, 2021, https://www.christianpost.com/news/the-renewal -aims-to-restore-americas-covenant-with-god.html.

4. Kevin Jessip and Troy Anderson, "Living in Prophetic Times," The Return, https://thereturn.org/living-in-prophetic-times.

5. Stacey Thoroughgood and Wendy Griffith, "Major Sign of Revival as Greg Laurie, Harvest Christian Fellowship Baptize 4,500 Souls at Pirates Cove," CBN, July 9, 2023, https://www2.cbn.com/news/cwn/major-sign-revival -greg-laurie-harvest-christian-fellowship-baptize-4500-souls-pirates.

6. Talia Wise, "TN MegaChurch Experiences 'Genuine Move of God' as 136 Get Spontaneously Baptized," CBN, August 14, 2023, https://www2.cbn .com/news/us/tn-megachurch-experiences-genuine-move-god-136-get -spontaneously-baptized.

7. Sean Feucht, "Sean Feucht's Brazen Worship Movement," CBN, December 10, 2022, https://www2.cbn.com/article/worship/sean-feuchts-brazen -worship-movement.